"What if you could peek inside the playbook of a championship sports team to see how they did it? That's what it feels like as you read *Lead Your Tribe*. A talented entrepreneur, Piyush shows his true gift as a great teacher by sharing his journey. With clever wit and a knack for storytelling, he illustrates firsthand how he built an exceptional culture. I was fortunate to spend some time with the team he built and can attest to their special bond. His formula clearly works."

—Mark C. Winters, co-author of *Rocket Fuel*

"When we started implementing these principles into our company, I saw productivity and morale increase dramatically. This book shows you how to build a better company—and a better life—by cultivating an atmosphere of communication."

—Kyle Green, Director of Film & Games Curriculum, Pluralsight

"How you interact with your staff drives your culture. Piyush has outlined the rules you need to follow to turn your business into a culture of excellence. The information in *Lead Your Tribe* changed the way I conduct business on a day-to-day basis. We all want a great culture and this book shows you how to build it."

—Dr. Justin Scott, Founder, Pure Dental Health

LEAD YOUR TRIBE, LOVE YOUR WORK.

LEAD
YOUR TRIBE,
LOVE
YOUR WORK.

An Entrepreneur's Guide to Creating a Culture that Matters

PIYUSH PATEL

Founder of Digital Tutors

DREAM **BIG**
IMPRINT

DREAM **BIG**
IMPRINT

5828 NW 135th St, Suite B
Oklahoma City, OK 73142
www.dreambigimprint.com

Book Jacket Design by Stephen Treadwell and Monkey C Media
Book Interior Design by Monkey C Media
Illustrations by Stephen Treadwell
Author Photo by Amy Gray

Printed in Canada

First edition

ISBN: 978-0-9986465-0-3 (hard cover)
978-0-9986465-1-0 (trade paperback)
978-0-9986465-2-7 (eBook)
978-0-9986465-3-4 (ePub

Library of Congress Control Number: 2017904940

TO THE MEN AND WOMEN OF DIGITAL-TUTORS

Thank you for the gift of being your leader. Your creativity and craftsmanship continue to humble me.

DEREK AND DAN

Thank you for making this project a reality.

LISA

My wife, business partner, best friend, and pen pal: thank you for trusting me and letting me drive the bus.

CONTENTS

MY JOURNEY (AND PROBABLY YOURS)

*ell, shit.*

I was only three years into what should've been the greatest entrepreneurial adventure of my life, and that was my conclusion.

I was screwed.

Damn—what have I gotten myself into?! It didn't take long for my life to get turned upside down. I guess that's nothing new for anyone who's quit their job, started a company, had a child, and moved to Oklahoma City, all inside of a few months.

It started when I was granted tenure as a college professor teaching digital animation less than a year after Nick was born. My immigrant parents were thrilled. My dad's voice echoed in my head, "You've got a government job. You'll get a pension. You're set forever!"

For the record, receiving tenure was something I'd worked hard to achieve and was a career goal. The reality was not the dream

I'd imagined, though. I struggled to pay the bills. I struggled to support my growing family. I struggled to find joy in the job I used to love. Receiving tenure should have been cause for celebration, but it seemed like a punch in the gut. Was this what the rest of my life would be like? I didn't know what the future held, but I knew something had to change.

So I jumped. One month after tenure, I quit my job and decided to work full-time on my company, Digital-Tutors, which I'd started only a few months earlier selling digital animation courses on CDs.

When my parents found out what I'd done, they were in shock. I can still hear my dad's initial reaction like it was yesterday: "What did you do?"

Seriously: what had we done?

Lisa, my wife, played a vital role in the new business, keeping the books and the paperwork. Two of my colleagues and closest friends, Kevin and Tina, also made the leap with us.

At first, everything went well. Even better than I could've hoped. I loved being in charge of my own work's destiny. I loved working with my wife and two of my best friends. I didn't mind the sixteen-hour days. I loved the adventure of being in business for myself, solving a need, and the affirmation that came with it.

As we grew, work increased and we brought on more great employees. I loved it so much that I didn't even notice when things at the office began to change.

Somewhere along the way, working those sixteen-hour days went from energizing to draining. I was stuck in the weeds and spent my days putting out fires. I hated the feeling of a noose around my neck. I hated trying to make ends meet and always worry-

**I loved being
in charge of
my own destiny.**

ing about meeting payroll. I began to hate going into the office. When I left my teaching position, it was a conscious decision. It was a tough choice Lisa and I had made together, but it's one I remember making. This was different. I couldn't point to a single decision as the trigger. The first few years of hard work getting Digital-Tutors off the ground all seemed to blur. Suddenly, I realized I was in way over my head. I had a lease on office space, vendors, insurance, and healthcare, not to mention the paychecks on which other people depended to support their families and pay their own mortgages.

As I reflected on how I'd gone from being a new father to becoming a tenured professor to starting my own company, it hit me: *What have I gotten myself into?!*

If you are reading this book, I'm sure you've had this feeling, too.

I couldn't just close up shop, lock the doors, and go home. What would I do? Go back to teaching? What would our employees do? They had believed in us, and had staked their careers on our vision. What about our customers who had come to depend on Digital-Tutors to refine the animation skills they needed to improve their own livelihoods? I'd already left the station at what was now a runaway train. I couldn't just hop off. I found myself trapped in a prison of my own making.

MY WAKE-UP CALL

Backed into a corner, I started looking anywhere I could for a way out. As often happens, I found it where I least expected: during a presentation I attended about company structure and governance. One line on a PowerPoint slide changed the course of my company and my life: "What are your company values?" I stared at it. When I thought of values, the first thing that came

I found myself trapped in a prison of my own making.

to mind was some form of motivational poster. You know what I'm talking about. They hang on the walls of corporate America. The passage of time slowly transforms them from a decoration to something no one notices as they walk by. But it bothered me that I couldn't answer the question for my company. Digital-Tutors was making money, but I was miserable, putting on weight, and growing more depressed each day. Could this be the first step to a solution? As the seminar continued, I kept turning that question over in my mind. What were our company values? What did our company stand for? What were my own values? What did Lisa and I stand for?

I called her during our lunch break and asked her to book a bed and breakfast for that night. We locked ourselves in and decided not to come home until we'd worked out our core values, both for our company and for our family.

FINDING OUR CORE VALUES

Although I didn't know it at the time, the result of our stay at that little B&B was the foundation for a massive change at Digital-Tutors. When Lisa and I returned to the office, we held a staff meeting to share our newly realized core values. We needed to make sure everyone in the company was on the same page. We called these core values the "Rules of Our Game" because they were the bare minimum for someone to play on our team. Really, business is just a simple game and once everyone knows how to play, we all start playing together. Over the next decade, we refined and clarified those values, but at their core they remained identical to the ones Lisa and I originally crafted all those years ago.

Before I share them though, I need to underscore that these are *ours*. Copying them won't work for you because yours will be different. They have to come from your heart and spirit.

What you're going to read in this book isn't about how you need to incorporate Digital-Tutors' values into your organization. It's about how our lives changed when we got explicit about what we believed in, and what happened when we lived by those rules—no matter what.

I hope the examples in this book inspire you to discover your own core values and to help you find the courage to stick by them, no matter what. Once you find your genuine, bedrock beliefs, you can transform your culture from daily survival (under which Digital-Tutors had been operating) into a thriving culture.

That said, here's the values we shared with our team:

1. **Service with passion is our competitive strategic advantage.** It is the product we sell. Deadlines and tasks will not be fulfilled merely because they must be completed, but because a personal commitment has been made to someone.

2. **We do more with less.** Doing the right thing the right way the first time is less about speed and more about the right mixture of accuracy and effectiveness.

3. **Fun creates loyalty.** We are about building strong relationships that go beyond the paycheck. The closeness we share as a group and the openness to share ideas and make a difference are all tied to how intimate we are as a group.

Those five values transformed my company from a place I hated to go into a place I loved to call home.

4. **Respect.** We will not tolerate disrespect for people or property.

5. **Embracing positive change** means we adjust our goals and mission in advance of or in response to constantly changing opportunities.

Those five values turned Digital-Tutors into an online training powerhouse, becoming one of the best in the world. We grew from a six-figure company to a seven-figure company, and then an eight-figure company. We went from a handful of employees to thirty-two full-time people and three hundred freelancers. And we did it all without incurring debt or the help of outside investors. We bootstrapped the whole company the whole way.

We grew from hundreds of users to over one-and-a-half million. Our students and teachers worked with some of the biggest names and projects in the computer graphics industry, from Pixar and Marvel's *The Avengers* to ESPN and J.J. Abrams—even the FBI and NASA.

But more importantly: those five values transformed my company from a place I hated to go into a place I loved to call home and that felt like family.

FINDING YOUR CORE VALUES

Your values are what make you tick. They're not something you can copy from the latest Harvard Business Review or pick up from a leadership book on *The New York Times* best seller list.

Values aren't some motivational one-liners that will magically transform your business. As an avid reader, I know we're all supposed to have core values. They're the things you put in your mission statement, your company vision; they are the guiding principles of your business; yada, yada, yada.

After my wake-up call, I started examining our company's core values for the first time. I got real and asked myself, "What are the rules? What would we never do under any circumstances? What truly matters to us?" These were also some of the questions Lisa and I asked in our impromptu retreat at that B&B. We had been so busy that we'd never taken the time to articulate what we believed.

Sure, we tried to be good people. We tried to treat our employees, customers, and suppliers right. We wanted to create high-quality experiences and products. We valued those things, but what did we ultimately stand for? More importantly, what wouldn't we tolerate?

As we searched for the answers, two key truths became clear. The first is that you can't make up your values. Values aren't some goals you want to achieve. They're not aspirational; they're not what you want your company to be one day. Rather, they are rooted in reality.

Your values are what you reflect in your actions and what you believe to be true. Your company values reflect the people who work for the company today, not some time in the future. The culture you already have in place—a.k.a. the "way things are done around here"—reflects your values. These daily decisions come from your underlying priorities.

In short, your values have nothing to do with whatever you came up with in your last corporate retreat (vision and mission statements) and then hung on a wall somewhere, to be forgotten. Your values are demonstrated every day in your organization through the actions of your employees and customers.

The second truth is that, as the owner and/or leader of a company, your own values become the company's values. Part of founding a company means pouring your heart and soul into it. You set the tone. You make the decisions. You sign the checks. You have the final say. Every time you make a choice, every time you interact with stakeholders you're shaping the culture of your brain child. As a company grows, though, it begins to take on a life of its own. Unless you make a conscious decision about staying true to your core beliefs—unless you know your limits— company culture can start running wild, like an untended garden or a neglected child.

I hadn't considered either of these two truths. Eventually, as the company's values started to deviate from my own, my passion started to wane. The less Digital-Tutors embodied my values, the less I liked it.

What does it look like when you don't live by your core values? These days, I love coaching and advising leadership teams. When meeting for the first time, my first question is, "What are your core values?" Inevitably, one I always hear is "quality." They say this, but when a customer shows up on their doorstep needing something quickly and they scramble to meet the deadline yet deliver an inferior product to do so, then "quality" is not a core value; it's just an empty promise.

Another common value often stated involves something around the idea of teamwork. If you say it's important but choose to keep a toxic employee because they're a hotshot, you clearly don't care about teamwork, do you? Values aren't something you declare; they're something you live.

YOUR TURN![1]

In basketball, everyone plays by the same rules. When a player makes a shot, no one questions the results; the player's team scores points. When a player goes out of bounds with the ball, everyone knows that's against the rules. Imagine the chaos if an athlete showed up to play basketball, only to find one player kicking the ball like a soccer player while another was hitting it with a hockey stick.

Before an athlete starts playing, they need to know up front which game they are playing and its rules. Just like athletes, your team members need to know the rules of how to play the game of business.

We called our values the "Rules of Our Game" because it set the expectations up front: "These are the rules we're going to play by. If you're not playing by these rules, you're not playing our game."

So how do you get started? There's something tactile about writing things down. It helps cement your thoughts into something you can visualize. Start by writing down the words you think describe your core values. Sleep on it for a few days as you try to narrow them down to just a handful. Give yourself time to think on them, and circle the ones that resonate with you.

- **What are the rules of your game?**

- **How will you communicate these rules?** (Please don't say a poster on the wall.)

- **How will you keep your rules at the top of everyone's mind every day?**

---

1 Leading a successful tribe requires a constant stream of small investments into your team's culture. Throughout the book I'll offer "Your Turn!" takeaways to help you start investing in the long-term health of your tribe.

Values aren't something you declare; they're something you live.

B.A.M.! 2

Putting our company values down on paper was the easy part. But values didn't give our company a goal to attain. As fundamental as values are, they were just part of the puzzle.

When looking for a teamwork metaphor for the cover of this book, geese came to mind. Many people are familiar with their flying "V" formation and how the lead goose divides the wind resistance so that flying is easier for each subsequent goose. But did you know that as the lead goose begins to tire, it drops back and another takes its place at the point, fighting the wind? The whole flock rotates, allowing the others to regain their strength while the rested ones take point.

Of course, geese aren't always flying. But they're always loyal to their flock. Without a second thought, parents will place themselves in harm's way to protect their young. Although the lead goose switches off while in flight, there's still a true leader, one to whom the flock looks to survive. Together, the flock will rear the young. Together, the flock will find food and shelter. Together, the flock will survive.

That's the flock's goal: to make it together.

This is true for humans as well. We're social animals. We live in groups. We're hardwired to interact. Biologically, we need each other to survive. We need a tribe.

Did you ever learn about psychologist Abraham Maslow's hierarchy of needs? Maslow ranked human needs from our most immediate priorities (which he placed at the bottom of a pyramid) to our most abstract needs (which he placed at the pyramid's peak). He said that our basic needs—food and shelter—should be addressed first. Similarly, when thinking about people's motivation at work, their most fundamental drive is to cover basic needs. They need a paycheck so they can buy food and provide for their families.

Maslow said after those basic needs are met that we, as social animals, need more. We need love/belonging, esteem, and self-actualization.

Our modern world gives us easy access to the basics. Most adults in developed countries spend their nights under a roof, can afford basic nutrition, and aren't under serious threat of being mauled by wild animals in their sleep. Whether your employees know it or not, once these basics are fulfilled, they look to the next level of the pyramid, and then the next. If you want a truly successful tribe, you must help them fulfill those needs.

We want to belong to something greater than ourselves

MEANING

AFFIRMATION

BELONGING

SAFETY & SECURITY

PHYSICAL NEEDS

BELONGING, AFFIRMATION, AND MEANING = B.A.M.

Every company provides a basic paycheck and safety. Few companies truly go further up Maslow's pyramid to meet their staff's needs.

- **Belonging: we want to be part of something.** We're hardwired to belong to groups. We want to belong to a tribe, something greater than ourselves. We want to identify with the people with whom we spend most of our day. But to feel like we belong to a company, there are a lot of foundational issues that must first be put in place.

- **Affirmation: we want to be individually recognized and appreciated in a way that means something to us.** We desire something that strikes a chord deep inside us…not a gift card that reads, "Thank you, [*write name here*]!"

- **Meaning: we want to know that what we do makes a difference.** Digital-Tutors sold online training for creative artists at $49 a month. What we ultimately did was change our customers' lives. We showed artists around the world how to channel their passion into something that could put food on the table, give them a career, and put them on a path to greater success. *That's* what Digital-Tutors did. That's what our employees saw. That's the mission we infused into our culture.

Each person in a group needs B.A.M. to function as a true tribe. At first, all I had were my five core values and a team of people I loved. One of my mentors, Michael "Smitty" Smith, had discovered the power of B.A.M as CEO of a paint manufacturer in my hometown of El Reno, Oklahoma, and he helped me see its value. His work and dedication in creating B.A.M. for his employees helped show me that we had created something amazing. We had created a tribe.

If you want to look forward to coming to work every morning, collaborate with a kick-ass team of co-workers who give their all every day, a die-hard following of customers and fans, and a wildly profitable business, then all you need is B.A.M.

YOUR TURN!

If this is the first time you've been introduced to the concept of B.A.M., know that there's power in tracking your progress—in knowing you're traveling down the right path to building a tribe to lead and work you love.

Question: what are you intentionally and consciously doing to make the people on your team feel a sense of belonging, to give your team members personal affirmation, and to give meaning to their work?

Write it down now, before you read any further. Once you're done with this book, reevaluate your answer.

We had created a tribe.

BELONGING 3

Right now, millions of people around the world are at some kind of sporting event. Most fans happily pour their time, money, and energy into supporting their team. The next time you watch a game, look in the stands to see what I mean. Whether it's the $100 team-licensed jersey, cheering for one team and booing the other, or chanting along with the crowd, everything about a sporting event is to get the fans to feel a sense of belonging. It's "us vs. them" or "good guys vs. bad guys."

When the team wins, it's a win for *us*. It's "when we won the championship." If the team loses, it's a coming together against opponents who defeated "us." It's "we'll get 'em next year."

Let's take a moment to reflect on this. How much of an influence do the fans *really* have on the team? Not much. Will they ever join the players on the field to play the game? Probably not. Yet you don't have to be a sports fan to know that there is an extremely powerful sense of belonging in sports—even when the fans didn't attend that college or even live in the same city as their team.

If a sports team can provide this for people who may never have the chance to participate in the game, imagine how powerful it is to offer a sense of belonging to your tribe—your company's players who are physically in the game.

MAKE YOUR OWN JERSEYS

How can you tell when someone belongs to a sports team? By their uniform. I'm not ashamed to say I stole this method of providing belonging from the sports world. At Digital-Tutors, we were a prototypical tech company when it came to clothing. We sat behind computers for most of the day, so people wore what they found comfortable. For most people, this meant jeans and a casual shirt (or just a T-shirt).

Periodically, I'd have new shirts, hats, or other Digital-Tutors-branded apparel made. It was always custom-made and usually designed by our in-house artists. Occasionally, you'd have a couple of people show up to work with the same shirt, but I made sure to have a range of shirts created so everyone could wear something unique. All different, yet all us. The cost of the clothing was negligible compared to how much belonging it added to the tribe. Soon, everyone wore a "team jersey," every single day.

Our clothing extended beyond my employees. Whenever we'd post a photo of our team members on social media, someone would usually ask where they could buy a DT hat or shirt. But I didn't sell our clothes online. The only way to get our exclusive gear was to be a part of the Digital-Tutors tribe—by being an employee, a vendor, an awesome client, or a power user.

Again, taking a page from sports teams that offer limited-edition apparel to commemorate special events, any time we hosted an event or traveled as a company, we always had custom shirts made for the event. We'd give these away for free. Rather than trying to turn us into a de facto clothing company, I was happy to front the cost of a bulk shirt order in exchange for building a stronger tribe with a great sense of belonging.

GO FOR THE GOLD

Olympic athletes don't win a gold medal with a shotgun approach. They focus on one sport and train to be the best. If you want to win a gold medal, you do one thing and you do it better than anyone else. A common misconception I come across when coaching a client is the idea that you must excel at a lot of things. They think they need to offer their product or service to a wide audience to be successful. This sort of shotgun approach can wreak havoc on your tribe members' sense of belonging.

I'd be lying if I said I'd never considered the idea of expanding beyond our niche in the creative space. I thought about going toe-to-toe with the online training platform Lynda.com. But that wasn't Digital-Tutors. We didn't want to make tutorials on how to use Gmail for the first time or how to program macros in Microsoft Excel. That wasn't us. It didn't ring true; it didn't give us B.A.M. We kept to our core mission: teaching people how to create digital animation for games and movies.

Over lunch, we argued about Batman vs. Superman, Xbox vs. PlayStation, and the quality of the visual effects on *Tron*. That's who we were. We stayed true to that…and so I always felt like we belonged right where we were.

HOW TO CREATE THAT SENSE OF BELONGING

Take a moment to think of a group to which you feel you belong. Maybe you belong to a church or a professional organization. Maybe it's your family or maybe a group of good friends. What are the actions that led you to feel a sense of belonging?

Perhaps it's the conference you attended for your professional organization. Maybe it was a great family vacation as a child or it was the chance to hang out and talk with your good friends every so often.

One of the greatest ways to build a sense of belonging is through shared experiences and the memories those create. So, you facilitate this for your tribe by providing those opportunities for your employees.

As our team expanded, so did the methods I used to help everyone feel a sense of community and kinship. We had company-wide experiences, like an annual trip for the entire team. I called them "Rock Star Road Trips," and for a few days I'd do my best to make my employees feel like actual rock stars, complete with luxury suites at sporting events and Michelin-star restaurants. These trips and outings were more than once-in-a-lifetime opportunities. They were shared experiences that my employees would talk about for weeks and years to come.

But belonging does not equal lavish road trips and expensive perks. There were also simpler experiences, such as Thai Thursdays, a weekly trip to a favorite restaurant over lunch. Week in, week out many of the same people would tag along for Thai Thursdays, forming a group of "regulars."

One of the greatest ways to build a sense of belonging is through shared experiences and the memories those create.

Another method that helped bring us together was our annual company dine-around. One night a year, a few team members would volunteer to host dinner at their respective homes. (The company covered the cost of the food.) Each host posted their menu for dinner and whether they had pets (for guests who might have allergies). Everyone else would sign up for a dinner they wanted to attend. This was an incredibly intimate way for people to get to know each other outside of work, especially for those with whom they may not have worked closely.

Not everything has to be done outside of the office walls, though. Every few weeks, usually at the end of the day on Friday, I'd call everyone together for a fun activity. Maybe we'd play a team-building game or maybe we'd just grab a beer in the break room as everyone went around and shared their big accomplishments for the week. I dubbed it "tea time" in honor of my parents' Indian/British roots, and it was a way to finish the week on a positive note. When you set up the framework for shared experiences, the people who share those experiences create memories they'll have together for the rest of their lives. For those who weren't part of these experiences, there's a sense of anticipation as they wait for the next chance to be part of it.

As we said earlier, creating a tribal culture is "the way we do things around here." Your real team is made up of the people who like the way you do things here and decide to stay. Culture isn't some buzzword. You can manufacture good products, but you can't manufacture good culture. You can't buy true loyalty. You can't walk in one day and dictate how people will act, think, and react. It isn't something you control. You can provide opportunities, but it has to grow naturally. Real culture comes from the heart.

YOUR TURN!

After you've covered your employees' basic needs, they need to feel a sense of belonging. One of the best ways to do this is to start setting up rituals for your tribe. What are some traditions you can start to establish? How can you and your employees find opportunities in which to participate that build that sense of belonging because they are shared experiences?

Here are a few ideas to get you started:

- **Dine-around or progressive dinner:** host an annual event where everyone in your company gets to participate.

- **Lunchtime traditions: find your own Thai Thursday.** It doesn't have to be Thai or on a Thursday, but initiate the ritual. Same day, every week for a few months. Invite others to tag along, but refrain from turning it into a business lunch. Use it as a chance to share experiences with your tribe.

- **Team jerseys: offer your tribe the chance to wear the same jersey.** Periodically have shirts, hats, or other apparel made for your team.

AFFIRMATION 4

Belonging to a tribe is one thing. Loving it is something else.

The first few times I gave someone a raise, this is how it went: Lisa and I would bring them into the conference room, sit them down, and say, "Stan, what a great job you've done over the past year. For all your awesome work, we're giving you a ten percent raise."

Whatever their salary, ten percent is a lot of money. I was elated to be able to give it to them. Not a one-time bonus. Not an appreciation gift. Not a token raise just to keep up with inflation. A real, honest-to-goodness, this-is-the lowest-salary-you'll-ever-make-here, permanent jump in their income.

I don't know what I expected from them. I know what I'd have done back in my teaching days if the president of the college had called me in and given me a ten percent raise. I'd have flipped over backward if they'd just given me a two percent raise!

What did our people do?

"Oh, wow. Thank you. Um, wow. That's great."

Silence accompanied by an awkward look on their face.

Then, "Did you need me for anything else?"

Disappointed, I'd say, "No, that's all. Just wanted to let you know about your new raise."

They'd thank me again and then go back to their desk.

I'd look at Lisa and say, "Well, that sucked."

I guess I wanted them to jump on the table and dance for joy. I thought they'd call their significant other and scream, "Honey, we got more money!"

Nope.

Just a somewhat embarrassed thank-you and a "Can I get back to work now?" I didn't feel like they understood the true significance of what it took to give them that raise. In a small business, every penny counts. More than that, I wanted this to mean something for them.

I came up with "raise dinners." Instead of giving a raise every year, I waited a year-and-a-half or even two years to give someone a raise. While $5,000 is a nice raise, getting $10,000 or $15,000 carries a much bigger punch. Instead of having them come into the conference room, Lisa and I would take them and their significant other out to a very nice dinner.

Our favorite place to hold these dinners was Mahogany Prime Steakhouse, an elegant restaurant with a wonderful ambiance: low lighting, natural wood and stone—just what you'd think of when you go out to a "nice place." We'd order steak dinners and talk about all the projects that were going on. But instead of talking to the employee, I'd talk to their partner.

I'd start with sharing important milestones their significant other had reached: "I really appreciated how James helped a key customer, who was a concept artist on *Star Wars,* solve a problem they were facing in production.

"Your husband helped us produce over thirty courses this year and covered topics which we had only dreamed of before he joined the company. Because of him, we will reach a huge milestone this year.

"Also, I just wanted to thank you for sharing James with us. I know you have three kids and I'm sure it's hard for you to be the main caregiver while he is at work having fun…but we really couldn't do this without him."

Then over dessert, I'd drop the news to our employee: "Lisa and I are so very thankful for all that you do and continue to do for us. We would like to give you a $15,000 raise. We understand that money isn't everything, but we want to let you know you mean a lot to us, and that we value you and what you bring to the company."

Boom.

After the shock, the tears, and/or the laughter, their partner would turn to my employee and say, "In the morning, I don't want to hear you hitting snooze—you go get your ass to work!"

What did having dinners accomplish? Financially, I was putting off a raise for an additional year, so nothing on that front. The cost of dinner was a negligible expense. But the value to the employee of having the owner brag on them to their significant other for a couple of hours, and then to let them be the hero bringing home another fifteen grand a year? Priceless.

What does this have to do with loving our tribe?

We affirmed the value of our employee in the eyes of their loved ones. We showered them with honest praise, and then put our money where our mouth was by giving them a shocking raise. We made them feel valued. We made them feel loved.

OUR MEETING RITUALS

Every month like clockwork, Digital-Tutors had our one and only recurring staff meeting.

Everyone left their phones behind and picked up pen and paper. We'd all gather around conference tables in a room where, for the next two hours or so, we'd reflect on what happened in the past month and look at what lay ahead in the next month. The core of the agenda was always the same:

- **Values stories: 60 minutes**

- **Updates from each team: 30 minutes**

- **Important dates and financials: 15 minutes**

- **Your big takeaway from the meeting: 15 minutes**

As you can see, the very first thing we did was go around the room for an hour and let each person share a story of witnessing another employee who exemplified one of our five values.

We affirmed the value of our employee in the eyes of their loved ones.

Let's stop for a second to consider the direct cost of that. If we had thirty-two people in that room and the average salary was $80,000, then that meeting would cost the company about $29,500 per year. That's just salary. That doesn't count the opportunity cost of engaging with customers, working with potential enterprise clients, creating marketing material, or anything else. Factor that in and you're talking about an additional several thousand dollars lost every month. And a good portion of that time would be sharing value stories. Was it worth it?

Absolutely.

The recipe for a great value story contained three key ingredients. First, it tied to a specific value. Therefore, before sharing a story, each person would mention the value their story related to.

For example, Andrew kicked off one meeting with this: "My story is about Linda and involves the value that **fun creates loyalty**. Last week, she invited a group of us to come over to her house to play board games. It was a great opportunity to get to know her and the others a lot better outside of the office."

The second ingredient for our value stories was to make sure it was for a specific person. When you have great people working for you, it can be tempting to share stories about more than one of them. For example, sharing how an entire team did something spectacular, but we always discouraged that. We wanted to shine the spotlight on a specific person who embodied our values.

Another time, Christian stood up. "My story is for Aaron and **embracing positive change**. For those of you who don't know, Aaron took on a new responsibility this month as he started creating some marketing videos. Last week, he streamlined the process for these videos and he also has volunteered to take on some of the other marketing videos as well."

Christian could have congratulated the entire marketing team for a job well done on the new videos. By talking about a specific person, he let Aaron know he noticed the hard work that he put into the new videos.

The final ingredient for a great value story is tying it to a specific event. It's not a general blanket statement. For example, Kevin might say, "My story is for Cory. The value is **service with a passion**, although I guess it could also fit into **doing more with less**. Cory's been working on a new feature for the site. Just before his deadline, I think it was a Tuesday, he found a couple of major bugs. Instead of releasing it first and fixing the bugs later, he was up here until ten o'clock that night 'squashing' bugs. He hit his deadline, and, in the weeks that followed, no customers have reported any issues!"

I'm sure Cory worked hard on the new feature for days or even weeks before his deadline, but instead of a story about the entire project's success, Kevin pinpointed a specific event. When Cory made the conscious decision not to release a buggy feature and then do what it took to fix the issues, he exhibited service with a passion—and Kevin's story affirmed that behavior.

As the company grew, so did the number of people sharing value stories. The monetary cost to the company would grow right along with it. But I knew it was worth it.

Of course, new hires usually wouldn't get it right away. When it came their turn, they'd often resort to giving someone a shout out: "I really liked how Jackson's latest course turned out. Great job, Jackson!"

As true as it may have been, that's not a great example of living Digital-Tutors' values. When this happened, I'd wait until after the meeting and pull the new hire aside, offering them some coaching on the three ingredients of a great value story for next month's meeting.

Practice makes perfect. So I'd ask their team leader to share value stories each morning. This repetition helped each person learn how to look for the values faster by learning from the right examples. It also offered new hires a chance to hear more experienced team members lead by example as they shared stories. As a bonus, it also helped the team grow closer to their new team member.

Without fail, by the next monthly meeting the new hire would offer a narrative with the key ingredients. It was a great way for our employees to affirm each other, it gave me a great opportunity to see how team members were doing, and it provided a chance to coach individuals on our values.

When I'd talk about this practice with my entrepreneurial friends in the Entrepreneurs' Organization (EO), I'd hear, "What?! You guys shut down for almost half a day? Every *month*?! And this isn't, like, a sales meeting? Just Kumbaya shit? Uh-uh. That's too much payroll sitting there doing nothing."

Here's what I asked them: what were they losing by *not* taking time every month to instill those core values? What was the cost of their employees all rowing the boat in different directions? How much did they lose on a regular basis fixing mistakes that never should have happened in the first place?

Think about it this way: if you owned a factory back in the 1900s, wouldn't you expect to shut down everything periodically? Cleaning out the dust traps, tightening up the loose gears and pulley belts, replacing worn out parts before they broke, finally greasing that squeaky wheel—performing basic maintenance and, ideally, preventive maintenance. Wouldn't you consider that necessary? Sure you would. That's just part and parcel of running heavy machinery every day.

**What were they
losing by not taking
time every month
to instill those core
values?**

So why in the intellectual property factories of the 21ˢᵗ century would you expect to run the factory lines on full blast every day without ever stopping? People aren't machines; the processes in your company may be intangible or even invisible, but they still exist. They exist in how your team works together and in the final product or service that goes out the proverbial door.

Our monthly meetings gave me the chance to check all the dials and gauges. I got to see how close to optimum my people were running and to do some "maintenance" when they were starting to drift away from center. Basically, quality control.

Deeper than that, though, it gave us all a chance to affirm not only our values but our significance to each other. I'd use the time to be transparent with the company's financials, what we had built for the month and, together, we'd identify any project bottlenecks. We weren't just doing our work; we were working together to make a difference.

WHEN HE WANTS ATTENTION AND SHE WANTS TO TALK

How many times have you heard "People don't quit jobs—they quit managers?"

"If only he would have thanked me—just once!—I would have stuck it out." Or, "They never told me I was doing a bad job, but they never told me I was doing a good job, either." Or simply, "I never felt appreciated."

When confronted with these types of statements, the managers in question often say, "I told them they were doing a good job all the time!" Truthfully, they may have...but not in a way that meant anything to the person getting the message. Here's a simple yet profound idea: how about we provide affirmation in a way that means something to each person?

In *The 5 Languages of Appreciation in the Workplace*, author Gary Chapman posits that there are five primary ways (or "languages") that demonstrate love...and each person's language is different:

1. **Words of affirmation, such as a verbal thank you or a handwritten note.**

2. **Acts of service, such as helping a co-worker with a project even though you don't have to.**

3. **Giving or receiving gifts, such as getting your friend their favorite candy bar or a cup of coffee.**

4. **Spending quality time, such as listening to your teammate for a few minutes, or taking time to have lunch or meeting for happy hour.**

5. **Appropriate physical touch, such as a pat on the back or a congratulatory handshake.**

Once I found Gary's book, I had everybody in the company take the online assessment to understand how they like to be individually affirmed. Basically, what makes them tick? Knowing how each participant prefers to be appreciated helped us be intentional in how we affirmed them and ensured that our actions meant something.

If words of affirmation weren't somebody's thing, it made sense why they might feel a bit uncomfortable if praised in a public setting such as our monthly meeting. On the other hand, if somebody keyed into acts of service, it made sense why they appreciated a co-worker closing out a task for them.

We're hardwired to look for affirmation in different ways. While any kind of affirmation is great, we started seeing exponential results when we focused on making sure that every person received the kind of appreciation that super-charged them.

LISTENING IS AN ACT OF AFFIRMATION

Anger and frustration are nothing more than unfulfilled expectations. You can get as deep as you want with that, but the root of all anger and frustration always comes down to the expectations of one person not being met by another. When people don't get what they expect, they get frustrated and, over time, angry.

At the heart of every productive conversation, there are two roles: storyteller and listener(s). One person speaks and another listens. In highly productive conversations, they may even switch parts.

Almost everyone knows the storyteller plays an important role in the conversation. After all, they speak, imparting their knowledge so that others can soak it in. While the storyteller's role is important, the listener's role is *critical* to the successful outcome of the conversation.

While explaining this to other leaders, I point out a situation that often comes up. We are usually aware of when there are two storytellers in a conversation; it often becomes very heated. What many don't realize is there is an even sneakier role that can be more counterproductive to a conversation: a "waiter."

A waiter is someone who pretends to be a listener, but instead is waiting for the storyteller to finish speaking so they can shift into the storyteller role.

We've all experienced it: you're speaking to someone, and as soon as you finish you can tell they weren't listening. They were just waiting for you to finish so they could relay what was on their mind.

As a listener, you can affirm the speaker in different ways. Non-verbal cues such as eye contact can go a long way, telling the storyteller you're mentally present and acknowledging what they're saying. Another great way is to repeat what you've heard or to ask insightful questions as soon as the storyteller is finished. By doing this, you're letting them know you were listening to what they were saying. This is a huge affirmation boost. A productive conversation isn't about making sure both the storyteller and listeners agree. It's about ensuring all expectations between the storyteller and listener are fulfilled, thereby avoiding anger and frustration. You also affirm that you, as the listener, "heard" the storyteller. This manages anger and frustration by ensuring the message the storyteller is trying to convey is the one the listener is receiving.

YOUR TURN!

Before everyone in your tribe can be expected to understand their roles in a conversation, they need to first know the roles. The concept of active listening as an act of affirmation is something that needs to be practiced. A lack of practice is where you'll start to have "waiters" creep into your tribe. In most cases, waiters don't know the difference between the role of a waiter and a listener. They *think* they're listening.

In a 1986 publication, University of Maine researcher Dr. Marisue Pickering narrowed down active listening to these ten skills:

1. **Attending, acknowledging: providing verbal or non-verbal awareness of the other; i.e., eye contact.**

2. **Restating, paraphrasing: responding to the person's basic verbal message.**

3. **Reflecting: reflecting feelings, experiences, or content that has been heard or perceived through cues.**

4. **Interpreting: offering a tentative interpretation about the other's feelings, desires, or meanings.**

5. **Summarizing, synthesizing: bringing together in some way feelings and experiences; providing a focus.**

6. **Probing: questioning in a supportive way that requests more information or that attempts to clear up confusion.**

7. **Giving feedback: sharing perceptions of the other's ideas or feelings; disclosing relevant personal information.**

8. **Supporting: showing warmth and caring in one's own individual way.**

9. **Checking perceptions: finding out if interpretations and perceptions are valid and accurate.**

10. **Being quiet: giving the other time to think as well as to talk.**

Run an exercise with a group of three. Assign each person a role. One will be the storyteller, another will be the listener, and the final person will be an observer. Set a timer for five minutes, and have the storyteller recount a story to the listener. The subject doesn't matter; it can be a made-up story. When the timer goes off, talk about the skills each person recognized. Start with the observer, and have them identify the skills from the list above. Then ask the same of the storyteller. How many did they pick up on? Finally, see which of these skills the listener thought they were using. How successful was the listener at affirming the storyteller? And, in turn, how successful was the storyteller in getting their message across to the listener?

Try switching up the roles and going again until everyone has had a chance. Are there differences the more times you run through the exercise?

Practice makes perfect. At Digital-Tutors, we found it was helpful to practice active listening on a regular basis. We'd introduce the concept in the first thirty days for new hires and do it at least once a quarter as a refresher for everyone. I relied on the team leads to know who needed the refreshers each quarter.

MEANING 5

One of the most common questions I get when mentoring revolves around "how to deal with millennials." It's a sentiment that's usually followed by something about entitlement, flexible schedules, or something perk-related. When you try to attract and retain great people, your perks may be enough to get them in the door, but finding meaning is how you get them to stay with you for the long haul.

Millennials don't want just a job and a paycheck.

Sure, they need those things, but they also need more than that. Millennials want to change the world and have their work mean something. They want to feel like they're part of something bigger and greater than themselves. It's common to all of us. It's in our DNA: we want to belong. We want to be affirmed. And we want to know that our work means something.

Fast food restaurant Chick-fil-A did a great job depicting meaning in their 2010 promotional video, *Every Life Has a Story*. The job may be making chicken sandwiches and throwing them in a bag, but offering a great experience to every customer *means* more than that. Chick-fil-A set out to connect to their customer's journey and take a role in helping them achieve their goals. Even if it's just having a chicken sandwich for lunch.

Like many tech companies, a good portion of the Digital-Tutors tribe were millennials. We hired so many great graduates of the University of Central Oklahoma (UCO) that I decided to endow a scholarship. Usually the recipients of those scholarships sent a thank-you note in the mail, but one May, a recipient—a Mongolian foreign exchange student named Ganbaatar—wanted to thank us in person.

My assistant scheduled an office tour for the young man. Normally I conducted the tours, but I had an unusually busy day, so she took him around in my stead.

At the end of the tour, she popped her head in my office to see if I could say hi before he left. I shook Ganbaatar's hand warmly and said, "Hey man, it's great to meet you!"

He didn't say anything. He just stood there.

After a moment's awkward silence, I said, "Do you have any questions I can answer?"

He shook his head no.

I said, "Okay, well—good luck!" And I went back to my office.

Later on, I felt really bad that I hadn't even given him five minutes of my time. I asked my assistant to reach out to him and set up a lunch.

When we met, I started off by apologizing. "I want to say I'm sorry for the other day. I didn't give you my full attention. I was having a busy day, but that's no excuse."

He said, "I'm sorry too. I just didn't know what to say. I didn't know it was Digital-Tutors."

He gave me his back story. In Mongolia, any kind of decent-paying job is hard to come by. Ganbaatar wanted to make a better life for his family by becoming a motion designer. Despite living in a large city, there were no design schools. While searching for resources to learn motion design, he discovered—you guessed it—Digital-Tutors. Through hard work and plenty of late nights, he learned how to animate in Adobe After Effects. His new-found skills landed him a job at a local TV broadcasting station as a motion designer. Ganbaatar saved part of his income to take English lessons, which allowed him to apply to art schools in the United States. A few years later, he applied and was accepted to the design school at UCO. He earned a bachelor's, racking up a slew of student awards, including our scholarship.

The disconnect was that the scholarship was given in the name of our parent company, PL Studios. It wasn't until Ganbaatar was walking through our lobby (moments before our awkward meeting) and saw the Digital-Tutors logo that he realized that, by a seemingly random act of fate, here he was, standing in the office of the very company that had started him down this fantastic journey.

The realization left him literally speechless.

Of course, his story left me speechless. We changed his life—his whole world as he knew it. I honestly didn't know what to say. All I could muster up was, "Oh, wow. Um, well, what can I do for you?"

He said he needed an internship to graduate. I was happy to oblige.

A few months later, Ganbaatar joined Digital-Tutors through our internship program. Of course, he was a first-rate designer. One of his projects was to create our onboarding care packages, which were used to help new employees integrate into our existing teams. But what he gave our team during his five-month internship was far more than just great work: he became the living, breathing symbol of how we were changing the world.

My team got to hear his story firsthand. They heard about the money he sent home to his family. He shared stories about the long nights of using our videos to teach himself the skills needed to be productive in his job. He told us about his future plans.

After that, when developers squashed bugs or built a new feature on a website, they weren't just coding—they were helping people like Ganbaatar learn a skill that could change their life. When customer service reps worked on endless streams of support tickets, they weren't just replying to faceless users—they were interacting with people like Ganbaatar who were putting in the time and effort to make a better life for themselves.

We weren't just selling training—we were helping people change their family tree forever.

BEING MEANINGFUL ON PURPOSE

We didn't deal with our customers face-to-face. So, it was always hard to get to know the people for whom we were working. Digital-Tutors didn't save dolphins or babies. We sold online subscriptions to professional training courses for $49 a month. That's it. And yet, if you were to ask any of our employees if Digital-Tutors changed the world, they would say without hesitation, "Absolutely!"

The evidence of this was the hundreds—thousands—of stories, thank-you notes, and more from users all over the world.

He became the living, breathing symbol of how we were changing the world.

Does it sound crazy to say that we changed the world? Maybe—but I absolutely believe we did. We changed people's lives. We helped people train for their dream careers or to update their résumé so that they could keep the job that supported their family. We helped students find a career in which they could excel at and open doors they only dreamed were possible. We equipped people in developing countries to earn incomes competitive with artists in developed nations.

Yes, we changed the world.

But that wasn't enough: our tribe needed to *know* that they were changing the world. That's why we collected these stories, then told and retold them. We encouraged everyone in the tribe to collect stories. These became our campfire stories and the legends of employees who transformed our customers' lives. New hires, freelance subcontractors, vendors, new enterprise customers—everybody heard about the software developer whose dream of becoming an artist became a reality after landing a job at a major game studio. We all cheered when we heard about the amazing feedback regarding our customer support team. They had provided training to a small startup studio that could pay us only after they got paid for their own projects.

When you were part of the Digital-Tutors tribe, I wanted you to know that you were making a difference. You were changing the world—one person at a time.

YOUR TRIBE IS BIGGER THAN YOUR BUSINESS

A year after I stepped away from Digital-Tutors, I took a trip with Kevin. He'd been my second employee when I started the company and I wanted to say thank you for his hard work.

I asked him, "What is on your bucket list?" He said Oktoberfest and Japan. So we started our adventure in Germany at Oktoberfest and ended in Osaka at an EO cocktail party.

At that party, a guy from Malaysia walked over and struck up a conversation. We chatted about my winery in Napa and made other small talk. One thing led to another and Kevin shared that he was in the digital animation industry.

The man said, "Oh, my daughter Kelly works in video games. Hang on." He motions across the room for her to join us.

I said, "Hi, Kelly, my name's Piyush Patel. I'm the founder of Digital-Tutors."

Her eyes widened, "Oh my god!"

Her dad turned to her. "Kelly, do you know Digital-Tutors?"

"Dad," she said, "*everybody* knows Digital-Tutors!"

For the next two days at that event, she sat with us at our table, joined us on our tour bus, and tagged along on whatever we were doing. She shared how much of an impact we had made on her schooling and career.

On the plane ride home, I turned to Kevin and said, "What are the chances? What are the chances that we'd just happen to be at a reception in Osaka and meet a man from Malaysia who introduces us to his daughter who lives in Singapore who used Digital-Tutors to get through game design school and get a job in gaming? How many other people like Kelly are out there?"

Here's an even better question: how many people are out there for whom belonging to a company's tribe actually *means* something?

Don't look at your company just for what it does. Sure, if you're a pharmaceuticals company, it's easy to find meaning in what you do: you save lives. But what if you lay flooring? What if you manufacture plastic bottles? What if you own a string of car washes? Meaning goes deeper than just what you do. Meaning goes down into the heart of why you do it.

The company is not the tribe. Your tribe may be centered or focused around your company, but it's about something more than just the commercial transaction.

Digital-Tutors was about much more than a subscription-based tutorial platform. Our customers became our raging fans and some of our greatest cheerleaders. It's because they were part of something bigger: our tribe.

THE 3 HAPPIES—CREATING DAILY B.A.M.

As a business owner, your challenge is to figure out how to help your tribe feel like they're part of a cohesive team, not just code and graphics churners (as in our case). There's just not enough time in the day to check in with each person individually. How can you create some unity and instill a sense of belonging, affirmation, and meaning (B.A.M)?

Since we worked with the cutting edge of technology, of course, we went old school: pens and Post-It notes. Every person would get a pad of Post-It notes. They were color coordinated by team; the marketing team would use yellow; the development team, green; customer service, blue; and so on. The colors themselves didn't matter as much as each team having a different one.

Every morning—and I do mean every morning—each team of five to eight people would take a few minutes to jot down three

Ashley   June 1

- Productive meeting with Jim discussing the updates to the website.

- Completed designing the logo for the new app.

- Taking my dog for a walk after dinner.

Stan

1. Great
   John ar
   of our

2. Fini
   repl
   hel

things that made them happy in the last twenty-four hours (or whenever they'd last been at work). Two had to be work-related; the third had to be personal. Each person would then read them out loud.

After everyone had read their 3 Happies to their team, the Post-Its would get stuck on the wall where everyone else would see them as they passed by to the bathroom or break room. It was old-school social media. It wasn't rocket science.

What those three little notes did for the Digital-Tutors tribe was create a sense of belonging. Everyone participated and the color coordination helped anyone passing by see who belonged to your team. They were using the same colors as everyone else on your team.

The 3 Happies also provided daily affirmation. Every day, each person would self-affirm exactly the things they *wanted* affirmed. Those few minutes every day, no matter what was discussed, spoke volumes to everyone. It said that their happiness was important to us. We wanted to hear about it.

YOUR TURN!

Before you can provide meaning, you need to know what offers meaning to your tribe. What are your team's dreams? Have you asked? What are the stories from your customers that you should be sharing with your staff? Make them legends—stories that can be passed on for months and years. The 3 Happies activity can be a great way to help your team provide B.A.M. to themselves, but also for you to get to know what provides B.A.M. for each person on your team.

To get started, gather everyone in your company and explain the rules of the 3 Happies. Commit to doing this for the next thirty days with your tribe.

Everyone writes their 3 Happies on a Post-It. First thing in the morning (before checking email or starting work), have everyone in your company share their 3 Happies with their personal team. After they're done, have a team leader collect them and hang the notes in a public space for the remainder of the day. At the end of the day, you (or someone you designate) can take them all down before heading home.

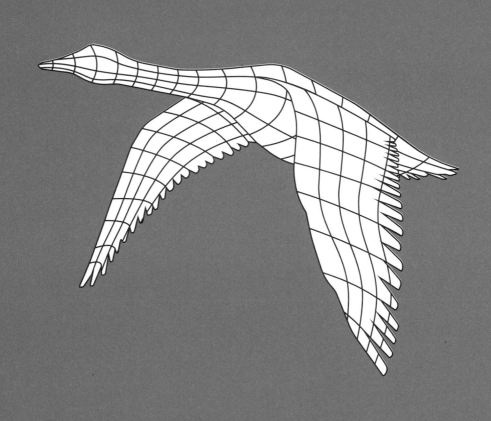

PLAY BY YOUR OWN RULES 6

A few years in, I felt I'd finally figured out how to play the game.

We knew how to manage our cash flow to keep the company healthy. We knew how to keep our customers happy. We knew how to stay in business and keep the doors open. We weren't stumbling around in the dark anymore. We had finally figured out how to run a successful business.

In reality, I was still a newcomer. I just did what felt right and what I saw other successful entrepreneurs doing. It never occurred to me that I could create my own playbook.

As I started to figure out how our core values and B.A.M. worked together, my leadership team and I made a promise to ourselves that those core values and beliefs would be our bedrock principles—the rules we would use to play by in our company and in our family.

It was our sandbox. We decided we'd play it our way or we wouldn't play at all. The same went for everyone else, from customers and employees to vendors: everybody played by our rules or they could take their toys and go home.

This didn't sit well with some people.

PUT YOUR MONEY WHERE YOUR MOUTH IS

Sticking to our guns cost us enormously in time, money, and lost opportunities. One of the biggest tests came when I heard that Claire, an account rep, was continually mistreated by Henry, who represented one of our largest enterprise customers. I went straight to Claire to find out what was going on. She admitted that she'd suffered in silence because a) she didn't want to whine, and b) because this customer accounted for a large portion of our gross revenues.

After listening to her, it was clear that not only did Henry continually mistreat her, but I suspected that he did so because he felt he could get away with it. As the vice-president of procurement for one of the largest companies in the world—a household name—I'm sure he felt like he could probably get away with murder.

I said, "You know what? The next time Henry calls, send him to my phone."

Claire said, "Are you sure?"

"Yes, I'd love to have a little chat."

Sure enough, he called a few days later. The receptionist knew to send him directly to me. I answered, "This is Piyush."

"Oh, um, Mr. Patel?"

"Yes?"

"Yeah, is Claire available?"

"No, Claire is not available, sir."

"Oh, okay then, I'll just try back."

I said, "No, you won't."

Silence.

"Umm, what?"

I said, "Yeah, here's how it works. We don't really need your business."

After swallowing his tongue, he came back in full force. "Excuse me? Do you realize who I am? I'm with—"

I cut him off. "Sir, we are Digital-Tutors. And guess what? There's a shit-ton of you guys needing my training and there's only one DT. And I'm not going to let you abuse my people.

"So here's what's going to happen: as of today, we're refunding all your money. No pro-rated bullshit: you're getting a full and complete refund. Also, as of today, we're cutting all your training. Your hundreds of employees online right now? Access revoked. You can explain your behavior to your shareholders. Don't call back."

Click.

I'd never done anything like that before. We bend over backward to accommodate our customers and serve our tribe. But after Claire related to me just how much abuse she'd put up with, it was an easy decision to make.

When I told Claire what I had done, she started to tear up. She was so relieved to know she didn't have to put up with that jerk anymore. She felt overwhelmed that she was important enough to Digital-Tutors—to me—that I would put her feelings ahead of our money.

This is the part where most business owners tell me I'm crazy. If you're hardcore, you could argue that I put one young woman's feelings ahead of the welfare of our entire company. You don't just slash revenue and not feel it. It affects everybody. I made a rash decision that could have eventually cost other people their jobs.

But I didn't fire that customer to make one employee feel better. I did it because he wasn't playing by our rules. When you don't stick to the rules, you automatically get disqualified. Go be an asshole in your own sandbox; you can't play in mine. We had made millions without that company, and I had faith that we could do it again.

A funny thing happened, though: the next morning, they called back. Except this time, it was Henry's boss.

"Um, yeah, we were wondering why we can't log into DT this morning? I'm getting flooded with emails from our employees that they can't get logged on?"

I said, "Oh, Henry didn't tell you?"

"Tell me what?"

"That he's been harassing his Digital-Tutors account rep without mercy, so I fired your company and refunded your money. You're no longer a customer of ours."

Stunned silence. "Oh! No, I had no idea! Well, um, what can we do to make this right?"

Go be an asshole in your own sandbox; you can't play in mine.

I said, "Okay, you want to make things right? Here's how we're going to do it. You're going to buy three years in advance, paid in full, up front. No corporate discount. Zero. And I don't want Henry calling here again. Ever."

Without missing a beat, he said, "Okay, sounds great. Please turn us back on."

And that was that.

Digital-Tutors wasn't a mammoth enterprise, nor were we one of Silicon Valley's fabled unicorns. I didn't have the clout or market position to get away with firing Henry's company. I wasn't planning on getting away with it. I just knew that I wasn't going to let them abuse one of my people. I couldn't say that one of my core values was "we will not tolerate the disrespect of people or property," and then allow precisely that to keep happening.

We didn't.

REAL CULTURE VS. FAUX CULTURE

I certainly didn't plan on being able to turn around and charge them full price for three years up front. But that's the benefit I reaped by being inflexible when it came to Digital-Tutors' core values. That payment, though, paled in comparison to what I reaped from my employees.

Can you imagine how Claire felt? Can you imagine how everyone else felt? To know that their boss went to bat for just one "lowly" account rep? To have hard proof that I had their back, no matter how big the customer?

That's what drives culture.

"Culture" doesn't mean providing free food and foosball tables. What good is a free meal if your designers and developers refuse to share it together? It's not about trying to imitate Google and Facebook by bringing in masseurs and having an in-house coffee bar. You can provide your employees all those things and still have a toxic culture.

Yes, Digital-Tutors had cool offices. We worked with a lot of creatives and studios, so we got all kinds of cool stuff for free: superhero action figures, movie posters, custom bobbleheads, and original artwork by some of the biggest names in entertainment.

Yes, we had free food and drinks. Yes, we took rock star road trips to Las Vegas, Denver, and Chicago. Yes, we paid exorbitant bonuses and gave out lavish Christmas gifts to our employees.

But none of that means anything if there's no real culture behind it. Those are just perks. Many people assume that great perks translate into a great culture, but that's not it at all. That's faux culture: it looks like the real thing, but if you scratch it you'll see that underneath, it's all fake.

At Digital-Tutors, we were *real*.

Many people assume that great perks translate into a great culture, but that's not it at all. That's faux culture.

YOUR TURN!

The moment you start drifting from your core values, your tribe will know it. Asking yourself tough questions only works if you're willing to give yourself truthful answers. You need to be genuine to who you truly are and have your core values reflect that. Here are a few things to think about:

- **Reflect on a story in the past year that tested your core values.** What did you do?

- **How do you describe your culture?** Does it fit with your core values? Why or why not?

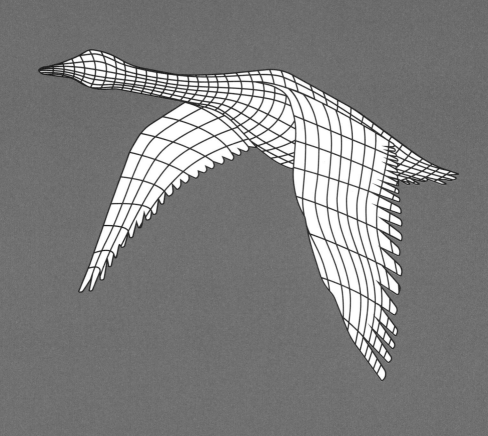

CULTURE IS ALL YOU'VE GOT

7

Owning a business is a roller coaster. It has highs and lows. Some you can see coming, some you can't. Don't get me wrong. The fact that we were making more money than this sixth-grade science teacher-turned-college professor-turned animator-turned-entrepreneur had ever dreamed of was amazing.

Little did I know it would soon come crashing down.

When I started the company, Digital-Tutors sold physical CDs with our training videos on them. We designed, printed, and shipped everything ourselves. That all changed in 2009 when I made the decision to shift our entire business model. Instead of selling CDs, we would sell an online subscription. It was a painful decision. Not everyone agreed, and there was plenty of pushback. We put stress on a lot of employee relationships. We even lost some good people who didn't think it was the right direction for the company.

Why had I been willing to take the risk? On the surface, everything appeared to be going well. But we were inefficient; we'd created a product that we couldn't produce at the pace we needed to to stay competitive.

We had to build a different solution, one that would allow us to have recurring revenue and was easier to use than CDs. In February, developers Tina and Jace started working on our online platform, codenamed *Bison* in honor of Digital-Tutors' Oklahoma roots and the Native American saying of "using all parts of the bison." After months of hard work and plenty of late nights and early mornings, we were ready to launch. On August 4, 2009, we flipped the switch.

Let's take a moment to consider the gravity of this. On August 3, we sold CDs—discs we'd shipped to thousands of customers around the world and from which we earned millions in revenue. In effect, the next day we fired every one of those customers. We no longer sold training via CD.

We were supposed to launch at 7 p.m. on the fourth, but things don't always go according to plan. As the clock neared midnight, it was down to one person: Jace, who was doing last-minute coding. There was nothing left for anyone else to do. After a few hours, we decided to give him some space. A few of us went to a tattoo parlor to commemorate the event.

I remember this like it was yesterday. When the artist asked which tattoo I wanted, I said, "I want a Bison and today's date."

"I've never tattooed today's date on anybody," she said. "What's so special about today?"

"Today, my world changes."

Shortly after midnight, Jace called to say Bison was live and we already had our first customer: an annual full-price subscription. What an emotional high!

Within a few weeks, that high was gone. The payment processor we had chosen was failing and our site kept breaking as a result. So we pulled the trigger on a new, top-of-the-line payment processor. But it wasn't an easy fix. Essentially, we had to rip out the entire back-end of the site and replace it.

More late nights, more hard work, and plenty more stress to go around. The future of the company, not to mention the livelihood of our families, was at stake. We'd spent hundreds of thousands of dollars on Bison, but despite all the technical debt, we couldn't sell the product until it was online.

By Christmas, the bulk of the work was done. There were bugs, but our site was no good to us if it wasn't live. This was before the summer of 2011, when Netflix announced its streaming plan, so the concept of an online subscription for videos required a lot of explanation for our customers.

For the next three months, Tina and Jace focused on fixing bugs. Across the office, Dana was fielding phone calls from frustrated and angry customers as she tried to explain everything from what an online video was to why nothing worked as it should.

MY SECOND WAKEUP CALL

At the time, I didn't see what was happening to our culture. I was so intent on recouping the hundreds of thousands of dollars we'd poured into making the switch that I was oblivious to anything outside my narrow focus.

In March 2010, Bison 2.0 was launched, with the major bugs fixed. Our subscription numbers started to increase almost immediately. I was so relieved that we'd pulled it off that I decided to celebrate by taking my small executive team on a long weekend to Napa Valley. The trip started off well as everyone enjoyed the chance to unwind after months of hard work. At dinner, we were in the middle of a toast when, seemingly out of nowhere, Dana broke down. "Are you okay? What's going on?" I asked.

"I...I can't work for you anymore."

The words hit me like a freight train. Here we were celebrating a major win. Our company was starting to make money again, and there's Dana, crying uncontrollably. Everyone in the restaurant started to take notice.

"W—what?" I stammered. "What do you mean you can't work for me anymore?"

"You've lost your way. I loved working for you. I loved what we believed in," she said through her tears. "And now, I feel like all you care about is revenue." After a pause, she said, "I just can't do this anymore."

I was speechless. Talk about a buzz kill. This was Friday; we still had activities planned for Saturday before heading home. The whole room was quiet. Everyone watched the train wreck unfolding in real time at my table.

My mind was racing. Did I actually exchange my values for money? I thought we had improved DT. We didn't have to carry inventory anymore; we could actually make some money now, and we could improve more people's lives with our training. It was more, more, more—but it was the *right* kind of more. Right?

Dana's emotions were contagious, and I was ripped out of my own thoughts as other people on my team starting to join in the tears. I didn't know what to do. *What the fuck is going on?*

Dana finally spoke. "I'll buy my own plane ticket and fly home tomorrow."

It was more, more, more—but was it the right kind of more?

"No," I said, "let's really think this through."

For the rest of the dinner, there wasn't a lot said. On the way out, Dana turned to me and said, "What did I just do?" Her voice started to quiver again, "I'm so sorry! I meant it—but I didn't mean to say it."

Fortunately, our hotel was nearby, so we walked back and I grabbed a bottle of wine from the desk clerk. We found a little bench and sat down.

I started, "What would make it right?"

She thought for a moment.

"First, you aren't about the customer anymore." She recalled our early days, before we had named our values, before we knew anything about B.A.M. "Back then, we were all about the customer. Now, after this new thing launched, the customer just isn't the priority anymore."

I knew what she was really saying: "*We* aren't your priority anymore." My tribe didn't come first. I wasn't taking care of them, so how could I expect them to take care of the customers? Dana and I talked for a long time about what had changed and how it used to be. Finally, I had an idea. "If I can make it better in the next sixty days, will you stay with the company?"

"Yeah, I'll stay." After a pause, she said, "As long as you don't fire me in the next sixty days."

I wasn't sure by the tone of her voice if she was being serious or trying to lighten the mood with a joke. I took it seriously. "I won't fire you," I replied. "The fact that you could tell me the truth is so much more valuable than anything else we've built. It means we've built something really special here."

After Dana left, I sat alone to let everything sink in. I took a sip of wine and emotions swept over me. I thought I had my shit together. I thought we were on top of the world. How in the world did I get to the point where my people were sitting at a fabulous dinner, crying about how things used to be? In the span of a couple hours, I'd gone from celebrating the success of a major product release with my exec team to sitting alone on a bench in front of a hotel in Yountville, California, feeling as if my world was falling apart.

I thought, *I am lying to myself about my ability to run a company with meaning. Here I thought everything was going great, and I didn't realize everything was falling apart. If Dana felt that way, I wonder if everybody feels that way?*

I'd had a taste of success, but at what cost?

That night was the catalyst. When I finally left that bench around two in the morning, I left with a new spark. I was determined to make one of the most badass companies in the world—and that change was going to start with our people.

YOUR PEOPLE ARE YOUR COMPANY

I was fortunate that Dana had a level of trust with us—with me—that she was willing to open up as she had. Digital-Tutors didn't have a monopoly on training for creative artists. We lived and worked in Oklahoma City. We certainly didn't have an abundance of choice when hiring from the small industry talent pool. Besides our core staff of thirty-two, we worked with over three hundred freelance subcontractors who could (and did) hire out their skills all over the world. We didn't have a capital advantage,

In today's economy, your most important assets get up and go home every night.

since we (proudly) had zero debt and zero investors. We didn't have a technological advantage; anyone can publish videos. We didn't have exclusive contracts with our customers; they could get their training from anybody, including free YouTube videos. In short, there was no piece of our puzzle that a competitor (or even a current employee) couldn't go out and copy.

Except culture.

You can't instantly create a network of relationships. You can't recreate the dynamics of a tight-knit group. You can't reproduce the social infrastructure and productivity of a team that already works beautifully together. Our culture is what attracted the best people to DT.

Over a few hundred years ago, the factories of the Industrial Age were massive. The start-up capital alone kept production in the hands of the über-rich. Who could afford to buy the enormous machines to run an assembly line but huge corporations?

Those days are long past. In today's economy, your most important assets get up and go home every night. Every morning, your product lines reassemble themselves to start churning out widgets (real or intangible) for your customers.

Some days, some parts and pieces of the production line don't show up. Some days, those assets even get up, walk out, go down the street, and walk into the doors of one of your competitors.

In nearly every industry, the barriers to entry have been swept away. As *New York Times'* journalist Tom Friedman says, "The world is flat," right? The only competitive advantage business owners can truly, wholly, and uniquely own anymore—if "own" even applies—is their company's culture.

If that's the case, you'd better make sure it's a culture that matters. As a business owner, you can create your own sandbox or company or whatever you want to call it. Culture is bigger than the sum of its parts.

I think of culture as the moat around my business. The more my culture matters...the more loyal my people are to me and my company...the deeper their relationships are with me and with each other...the deeper and wider the moat gets around my business and the harder it is for the competition to hire my talent away (not to mention the fact that it makes my people reluctant to leave in the first place).

Putting all other considerations aside and focusing purely on business strategy, your culture is the only thing your competition can't copy. They can copy your technology, your methods, your warehouses, your kitschy offices, your HR policies, and your ideas.

They can't copy how your company makes your tribe feel.

YOUR TURN!

Is your leadership team telling you what you want to hear, or what you *need* to hear? Trying to get to the core of how your tribe really feels can be tough. If you're lucky, you'll have someone like Dana who will tell you what you need to hear. Here's a handy exercise you can use to get past the people who are telling you what they think you want to hear.

At least once or twice a week, make a point to have a face-to-face conversation with people around your office to get a pulse on your culture. It doesn't have to be everyone, and it doesn't have to be the same people each time. Here are a few questions you can use as a framework for your conversation:

- **What's the one thing that makes our culture unique?**

- **Why do you come to work each day?**

- **What's one thing we should *never* stop doing?**

- **What's one thing we *should* stop doing?**

To gain someone's trust, you must offer your trust first. Allow yourself to be vulnerable first, and they'll be more likely to open up to you. Sometimes all it takes is affording someone the opportunity to let you know what they really think.

The most important thing! Don't talk—just listen and say thank you for sharing. Don't try to defend or fix the topics brought up.

LIVING YOUR VALUES NOW 8

When taking on a new coaching client, a red flag goes off in my head when they say, "Okay, these are what I want my core values to be." They've lost the game before it's even begun.

You can't wish for values or hope for them in your company. They're not some words hanging in a pretty frame on your office wall. If they are, they're useless. Your values aren't something you visit every year at the corporate retreat, only to shove back into a dusty desk drawer until next year. Those kinds of "values" are lifeless. They're not something you decide or declare; they're something you discover. They're what guide you every moment of every day. Your core values can't be aspirational, something you hope to reach at some point.

You can work on being great later. First, you need to find out who you are now. Figure out what you value and what rules you wouldn't break under any circumstances. Then get explicit about those rules.

Values are not something you decide or declare; they're something you discover.

Share these rules and values throughout your company. Measure every decision and every dollar against them. Find your unyielding inner leader and stick to your guns, no matter what. Make sure your values address belonging, affirmation, and meaning: the core needs of not only your team members, but their loved ones, your customers, your suppliers, your advisors, your investors, your board of directors, the pizza delivery guy, and everyone else even remotely connected to your tribe.

After my heart-to-heart with Dana on the bench, I learned the hard way that it's all too easy to lose sight of your values without realizing it. It was only because I had promised my people that "the company would operate according to these values" that Dana was able to call me out on losing sight of them. If she hadn't, it would have been just a matter of time before I fell back into the same rut as when I started Digital-Tutors: headed down the path to yet another *oh shit!* moment.

Because of our core values, I was able to see where things went wrong—how far we had drifted away from our path—and only then could I make things right.

I've shared what my five core values are so you'll be able to connect the dots on how my values influenced my decisions at Digital-Tutors. For your company, my values are not what's important. What's important is that I had them, I lived them, and I made a promise to myself and everyone around me that I wouldn't break them under any circumstances. Just as you have values, live them and hold them under any circumstance.

Your core values won't be the same as mine. They can't be. You have a different mission. Your company focuses on different outcomes. Your leadership style is different. Tribal culture is like a fingerprint: no two are identical. Your tribe members all have different abilities and unique experiences. They have different dynamics, different ways of getting the job done, and different goals. Whether you're a mammoth enterprise, a scrappy startup, or a Main Street mom-and-pop shop, it doesn't matter. What matters is knowing who you are and refusing to compromise.

THE BATHROOM BANDIT

You've been there: in the bathroom at that crucial moment when you reach for the toilet paper...and all you see is cardboard. You're in one of your most vulnerable positions and the person before you didn't replace the roll.

When I see an empty toilet paper holder, I see my core value broken: respect. When you use the last piece of toilet paper, you know it. In fact, you were praying there would be enough so that you wouldn't find yourself in a bad situation. So, you sat atop the porcelain throne, used the very last of the toilet paper, looked at the empty roll, and made a conscious decision: screw the next guy. You got what you needed. The next person who comes in will suffer some indignity because you didn't care enough about them to take five seconds to replace the paper.

At Digital-Tutors, I always believed that if we took care of each other, taking care of the customer would be automatic. I didn't have to teach the basics of customer service if our team practiced it with each other first. After several weeks of seeing empty rolls in bathroom stalls, it finally hit me that not replacing the toilet paper violated our core value of respect. I called everyone into our meeting room to discuss the "Bathroom Bandit."

I said, "I don't care who you are: that's disrespect. If you're willing to blatantly avoid helping out your fellow co-worker in the bathroom, then what are you doing during the workday when we can't see what you're doing? Do you need to be watched every moment so that we know you're doing the right thing? In how many other little ways are you pulling your team down in the long term?

"This isn't a daycare. Your mom doesn't work here. We're all adults and we know what's right. If we can't trust you on something as basic as replacing the toilet paper in the bathroom, then you don't belong here. Test me on it. Let me go into the bathroom after you and find the toilet paper's empty. It'll be your last day at Digital-Tutors."

My team knew that I never made threats like that. Feeling safe is one of the most basic human needs on Maslow's hierarchy (in the workplace, that translates as job security). I never joked or threatened people's jobs.

Because it was so out of character for me, everybody was like, "Aw, c'mon, Piyush. You're just upset. You wouldn't really."

I said, "Try me. If you don't have the respect to take care of your fellow team member on something as basic as toilet paper, you'll backstab them in the workplace all day long. You don't deserve the opportunity to be a part of our team."

That wasn't the end of it. The villainous Bathroom Bandit struck again. As crazy as it sounds, toilet paper became my litmus test. If I walked into the bathroom and found the roll empty (I never did catch anyone), I knew there would be issues in our pipeline. Sure enough, as the day went on, it would come out: a missed deadline, a co-worker problem, a communication issue…inevitably, something weird or bad had happened.

On the other hand, if there were no sightings of the Bathroom Bandit, it usually meant things were flowing. (Poor choice of

**Feeling safe
is one of the
most basic
human needs.**

words.) People were getting along, projects were getting done, and customers were happy.

Stocking the toilet paper isn't the point. Here's your takeaway: being inflexible on something as stupid as toilet paper reinforced the core value of respect and resulted in employees taking care of each other in all aspects of work.

Now, let's talk about another core value: Doing more with less.

GUERILLA TRADESHOWS

Like most startups, in the early days of Digital-Tutors, we were strapped for cash. However, when we had the opportunity to attend SIGGRAPH, the CG industry's largest annual conference at the time, I knew it'd be a huge boost for our business. I also knew we couldn't afford it.

First, there was the rent for the booth's floor space: "For $30,000 you get to use this square of concrete right here. Enjoy it." Since you don't want it to look like a patch of bare concrete, you have to spend the money to fix it up, right? That means a professionally-designed booth, super-nice tables, shiny hardware, the special mats to hide the extension cords—it has to look like you took time to build it. But, of course, it's something you had to build off-site, ship, and then reassemble at the show.

Check that. You couldn't do it yourself. By contract, you had to hire on-site labor at an exorbitant fee, one person for each of your own people working. At DT, we were used to putting in a lot of elbow grease to get things perfect. Hiring two or three laborers would blow through our meager booth budget. We had to find a workaround.

One of our core values was doing more with less. Figuring out how to create something amazing on a shoestring budget was a challenge for which we had practiced in thousands of little ways. This was a chance to really put our practice to the test.

Kevin and I flew in the night before, ahead of the rest of the team. We piddled around the tradeshow floor, unpacked some pallets, moved some cardboard boxes from one spot to another, and generally looked like we were loafing around. (We were.) As soon as the last laborer left and it was just us and the security guards, I looked at him, we laughed, and then we got to work.

We busted open our boxes hiding all of our supplies: snap-together framework, tables, and lots and lots of Velcro vinyl coverings. The table coverings were not expensive—they just looked like they were. The booth was as clean and minimalist as an Apple store. The one thing we did pay for was to have the tradeshow hang a 125-foot, bright orange banner above our space. You could see it from anywhere in the convention hall.

It looked awesome.

Early the first day, we gave away hundreds of free T-shirts to passersby in a bright orange, Digital-Tutors bag. Each time, we'd say, "Hi, nice to meet you. Here's a free T-shirt! Over the next three days we're giving away Xboxes, PlayStations, tablets, and all kinds of cool stuff, you can win, but here's the catch: each day, you have to be here in the morning with your Digital-Tutors T-shirt on. See you then!"

When people started pouring into the tradeshow, the first thing they saw was the bright orange Digital-Tutors banner perched high above everybody else's booths. As they walked around, they saw everybody carrying bright orange Digital-Tutors bags (not knowing those people hadn't bought anything; they'd just gotten a free T-shirt). On the following days, they'd see dozens upon dozens of people walking around with bright orange Digital-Tutors T-shirts on—the exact same T-shirts as our staff. It looked like half the hall were DT employees. When they finally came to our booth, it looked like the biggest one in the whole place. We had an enormous presence—at just a fraction of the cost of the other tech giants there.

One of our competitors said, "Wow, you guys are all over this place! How many staff did you have? You're like the Walmart of our industry! We can't even compete against you guys!"

That's doing more with less.

If we hadn't had that core value, do you think we'd have come up with that kind of guerrilla marketing? There were other startups there on a shoestring budget—and it showed. They could have done the same things we did. But doing more with less wasn't in their company's DNA.

"Do more with less" wasn't just a saying for us. It was something we lived. It was something that had been instilled in me as a teenager working side-by-side with my mother, cleaning up after guests and changing the sheets on the beds in my parent's motel in Oklahoma.

In running my own company, I didn't mind spending money. Compared to our competitors, we spent extravagant amounts on appreciation trips, gifts, bonuses, and the like. The goal wasn't to just save money but to also maximize the dollar and stretch it as far as we could. It was about being able to achieve more of whatever—time, clients, sales, quality, awards, tasks—with less of whatever: time, expenses, workforce.

We wanted to wring every last cent's worth out of every last dollar.

They could have done the same things we did. But doing more with less wasn't in their company's DNA.

YOUR TURN!

You're already living your values, and by extension they should already be a part of what you're doing in your company, even if you haven't taken the time to write down *how* your values are impacting your company. There's power in making conscious decisions around them so you can clarify the expectations with your tribe. This can mean some up-front work on your part to connect the dots.

- **On a sheet of paper, write down some of the events or activities you do at your company.** They don't have to be in order, just the first activities that come to mind.

- **Next to each event, write down the value that event or activity embodies next to it and why you think it embodies that value.** What are the key reasons you picked that value to be associated with that event?

Remember, it's possible (even likely) that some events or activities are negatively associated with one of your values. For example, not everything I did at Digital-Tutors embodied doing more with less, but this handy little exercise helped me to take a step back and confirm in my mind the reasons why I should or should not keep doing each one.

Repeat this activity periodically to help identify and affirm for yourself the things you should keep doing in your company, and the things you should stop doing.

HIRING 9

How did we find new people to join the Digital-Tutors family?

Did we do something über cool, like create a program that crawled across social media, DARPA, and the Darknet to find brilliant instructors, developers, marketers, and customer service people? Did we raid our competitors' talent pool? Did we design awesome animated ads and post them around the net? Did we pay headhunters to search out the perfect candidate?

If we truly believed that finding not just talent but the right talent—people who matched our core values—was so fundamental to our success, how much money do you think we slated for employee acquisition? If just one person could earn the company a half-million in gross revenue, how much of that were we willing to invest to find them?

Exactly $0.

Call me crazy, but I never had a plan for finding new hires. That might be because I never had a problem finding great people. Our company—our tribe—just seemed to attract them. One time, a guy stopped by the office and asked if we were hiring. We didn't have a receptionist then, so it was Rob who answered the door. He told the guy we didn't have any open spots, but he was welcome to leave his résumé.

That happens in every company. People stop by all the time to leave generic CVs or mass email those I-can-learn-anything-please-give-me-a-chance types of résumés. Not this guy. He knew exactly what Digital-Tutors did, knew exactly what kind of talent we looked for, and knew exactly how to cut through the crap to get to the good stuff. He was already on the fringes of our tribe.

He told Rob, "Well, I don't really have a résumé, but I have my demo reel. Can I leave that?"

"Sure." A minute later, Rob walked down to my office and said, "Piyush, just had a guy drop off his demo reel. Want to see it?"

Not particularly busy, I said, "Okay, let's have a look." I popped it in. And I was floored. This guy had incredible skills. I knew we had to have him. I jumped up and ran to the front. "Did that guy leave his number? Call him back! Tell him to turn around!" A few days and a vetting process later, he came on board.

Virtually every one of our hires came from inside the tribe: students from the local college, former customers who loved our training, and freelancers who came on full time. Most of our new hires, however, just came from employee recommendations.

Did our team members push some names that we didn't consider strong candidates? Sure. Did we hire somebody just because they were somebody's friend? No. Before you worry about nepotism, the good-ol'-boy network, and severely limiting our potential talent pool, consider this: who else better knew the caliber of work and the type of person Digital-Tutors needed? Who else better to evangelize our brand? Who else better to serve as our recruiting poster? Who else better to advertise our company? When you've built a culture that offers B.A.M., your people will want to protect it and promote it as much as you do.

Still, whenever I hired someone, I had to make sure they were a good fit. I didn't hire based on skill (though I certainly hired for aptitude). I figured no matter what someone's technical expertise, they were going to need more training. The VFX and gaming industries changed so quickly that whatever someone knew two years ago was probably moot. Instead, I looked for "one of us."

If I was willing to fire someone over whether or not they would disrespect their co-workers by leaving the toilet paper empty, I for sure would hire based on our core values. Interestingly, this meant some of our best people came from nontraditional or even unconventional backgrounds.

Christina, our first graphic designer, was referred to us by her husband…an electrician who came to fix an office lighting problem. He mentioned in passing that his wife was interested in graphics—despite the fact that she was then a pastry chef. Fast forward about a year, and Christina was on our team. Yup: a baker-turned-graphic designer. Her own personal values lined up with our values perfectly, she was a fast learner, and became someone our team relied on to crank out thousands of images for our site on any given week.

She wasn't the only one. We also had talented people like Brad, our writer for the Digital-Tutors blog, who was a culinary expert and college professor. Dana, whom I've mentioned before, had been a flight attendant for Delta.

Did incredibly talented artists apply to work at Digital-Tutors? All the time. Did we hire those talented artists? Only if they fit our values. No matter how much talent you have in a room, I promise that people working together as an effective team will beat a group of individualistic hotshots every day of the week. I didn't need people who were the most skilled in their field. I looked for great people who would sync with the rest of the Digital-Tutors family.

I looked for people who already believed in our values.

WHY YOU DIDN'T WANT TO WORK FOR DIGITAL-TUTORS

Every company has drawbacks to working there. Digital-Tutors was no exception. For us, though, I saw these drawbacks as advantages in attracting the people I wanted.

Reason #1: We were located in Oklahoma City. Don't get me wrong: I love my Midwest roots and OKC is home, but the fly-over states don't appeal much to animators on either coast. Once we got some traction, I could have moved our offices to somewhere with a bigger tech scene and talent pool, like L.A., San Francisco, Seattle, or even a little closer to home in Austin, Texas.

Why didn't I? Because it wasn't where our tribe belonged. Oklahoma birthed us, nurtured us, and was home to us. We weren't going anywhere. And we never had to. Artists working on movies are used to a fast-paced career of hopping from contract to contract and studio to studio. Those blockbuster movie projects often demand eighty- and ninety-hour workweeks or more. (I remember one potential hire touring the office and asking, "Where are the cots?" He thought we had hidden them for his sake.) On top

No matter how much talent you have in a room, I promise that people working together as an effective team will beat a group of individualistic hotshots every day of the week.

of the long hours, once your part of the project is done, you have to find another movie to work on. You might be out of work for two or three months or longer before you were picked up. That kind of feast-or-famine work schedule can play havoc with your life, especially if you have a family.

That's where our advantage was. At Digital-Tutors, all employees were full-time so as an employee you didn't have to worry about whether you would have a job in six months or not. You got an above-market salary which went even further, thanks to the much lower cost of living in OKC.

Reason #2: We didn't work on movies or games directly; we taught people how to work on movies and games. One of the big reasons why people get into movies and games initially is to have their name in the credits. This reasoning usually wears off after they get a few credits under their belt, but there's always the glitz and glamour of being able to see your latest DreamWorks Animation project on the big screen or brag that you were working on the latest Blizzard Entertainment or Lucasfilm project.

Again, this became another competitive advantage for us. Not everyone has the desire to see their name in the credits. They'd prefer to work on a range of projects. Instead of working on a single movie or game for years at a time, we worked closely with people who were making *all* of the latest blockbuster movies and games, all at the same time. This ensured that no two days were the same, offering a wide range of creative challenges that our team loved to tackle.

Reason #3: We were a small company. For most employees, that meant fewer (perceived) corporate perks, more (perceived) volatility, and fewer (perceived) opportunities for advancement. (Of course the flip side was less office politics, less corporate red tape, more action, and a greater personal impact. Difficult tradeoff, right?)

This kind of life didn't appeal to everyone. But that was the beauty of it. The people who wouldn't have been a long-term fit for Digital-Tutors never started at our company in the first place. The people to whom our pace appealed loved the fact that they could feel B.A.M., love their co-workers, and have a life outside of the job.

For people who had talent but also wanted a life outside the office, do you think ninety-hour workweeks appealed to them? Do you think they looked forward to jumping from job to job—and maybe even city to city—every nine months as they chased new projects?

I'm not saying you need to move to Oklahoma City if you want to have a great tribe inside your company. I'm just saying that if your everyday business aligns with your core values, then use what you have as a competitive advantage by adding B.A.M.

We didn't let our location or size limit us. We did what came naturally for us and attracted people who shared our core values. Our team members loved what they did, loved their co-workers, and loved where they worked.

YOUR TURN!

Finding top talent is challenging. Finding top talent *that fits your tribe* is crucial. How can you identify the ways to find top talent that fits in your tribe? Why not ask the people who have already gone through the process? Ask some of your team to think back to when they were hired.

Here are a few questions to get you started:

- **What were the reasons why you didn't want to work here?**

- **What was the key deciding factor that ultimately made you accept the position here?**

- **What gave you second thoughts about working here?**

- **Was there anything you were afraid to bring up when you first got hired, because you were the "new person?"**

Finding top talent is challenging. Finding top talent that fits your tribe is crucial.

ONBOARDING 10

Have you ever been lost in an airport in an unfamiliar city?

Your connecting flight spits you out, you're herded off the plane, go up the ramp, and fall out into the gate waiting lounge. You know you have to claim your luggage and then find your way to the rental car facility. What do you do?

Follow the signs, of course.

But what if there were no signs? What if no maps were posted? What if no maps existed anywhere? There's a din of noise around you, throngs of people sitting, milling, rushing…but no one's there to help you. They all have their own problems. If you're like most people, you're too embarrassed to approach someone and admit you're lost. (That's not until later, when you're sick and tired and still lost.) You wander around the airport, navigating by best guess. Maybe you'll eventually end up at the baggage claim… only to discover that you're so late that your luggage has been moved to the unclaimed baggage office.

That's how it feels like on the first day of the job at virtually every company. You get hired, you report for your first day on the job, your "trainer" shows you your desk, gives you a stack of HR papers to fill out, and says, "Hey, good luck! Let me know if you need anything!" And then they're gone. You sit there, staring at your stack of forms, wondering what the hell you're supposed to do now.

Eventually, you figure out how things work in the office…after screwing up a lot, being embarrassed by your basic ignorance, and getting your hands slapped for doing things the wrong way (although no one ever bothered to show you the right way).

All the dysfunction with none of the fun.

HOW TO MAKE NEW MEMBERS FEEL LIKE THEY ALREADY BELONG

You can feel the nervousness from *Disrupted* author Dan Lyons as he explains what it was like to arrive at HubSpot on his first day. His emotional roller coaster goes from the shock of losing a job to the excitement and fear of stepping outside his comfort zone to utter disappointment as he starts to realize his new company isn't as excited about his joining the team as he thought it was. His disappointment resonates throughout the entire book, making you wonder what might've been different if he'd felt welcomed on his first day.

Here's a radical idea: what if you welcomed new employees by making them feel, well…welcomed? What if new employees felt like they were wanted, appreciated, planned for, and important? What if the first day on the job was one of their best days on the job? What if they ended the day knowing exactly how things worked, felt like they'd found their niche, and came to work the next day on fire to get started? What if by their second day on the job, they were already doing some amazing stuff?

Honestly? It's not that hard.

Here's how we came to do it at Digital-Tutors. Two weeks before your first day, we'd mail you an inconspicuous black box (which Ganbaatar had designed for us). First off, who doesn't love getting goodies in the mail? In the box, you would find all your HR forms so you could fill them out at your leisure instead of spending your first day on the job filling out boring paperwork. You'd also find a slim book about Digital-Tutors: who we were, our history, photos of our team, our stories, and other meaningful content that helped you feel like you already knew us. We'd include a bright orange Digital-Tutors T-shirt. This would eliminate the fear of what to wear on your first day while helping you feel like you were already a part of the team the first time you walked into the office.

What we found people loved most was the bright orange picture frame we'd included. We attached a printed note to it that encouraged you to put a picture of your family or friends in it, then bring it to work when you started. That way, your desk would be personalized from day one. You'd also get a bright orange notebook and a pen (because when you went into any meeting, you needed to be ready to take notes; when we met, we didn't waste time— we got shit done). Lastly, we'd send them one of my favorite books, *Leaders Eat Last* by Simon Sinek. His book captured our approach to the way we did things. True leaders make sure that everyone else gets fed before they serve themselves. We wanted to make sure our new hires understood our value system.

Let me stop here to point out that doing a new-hire box didn't come from us sitting around trying to figure out how to get more out of new members of our tribe. It was a gesture that arose naturally from our desire to welcome the tribe's newest members. Imagine my surprise when I attended a business management course on the campus of MIT and found that, out of sixty-plus CEOs in the room, only a few did anything remotely like this for their new hires. I was the small fry in the room, yet I saw guys from mega-corporations taking notes as I outlined our fairly simple process: "Oh, a picture frame? That's good!" I thought at first they were joking, but I realized no one was laughing. It wasn't rocket science; we just wanted to make the new employee feel at home on their first day. It was the ingrained culture of welcoming a new member of our tribe vs. "Oh, hey. Here's your desk."

On your first day at Digital-Tutors, I'd spend the entire morning with you. I wanted you to hear straight from the founder what was important, what we believed, why we did what we did, and how we were going to change the world of online learning. I'd take you around to all the teams and personally introduce you to them, point out a lot of the projects on which we had worked or were working on, and take you out to lunch to talk about how we handled conflicts.

As we grew, devoting half of my entire day to a new hire became more difficult. What if I was busy that day? I'd move those other meetings. The most important investment was in people. If I couldn't make time, it signaled to them that they weren't that important. In the long run, starting out new people on the right foot paid dividends in motivation, buy-in, and teamwork.

HELPING YOU NAVIGATE YOUR FIRST MONTH

No one settles into a new company in a single day. Your entire first month was something on which we heavily focused on at Digital-Tutors to help you feel comfortable. When we were smaller, I'd ask someone to be your mentor; someone to help you fit into the tribe.

As we grew, this turned into a team of volunteers. The mentors were there to bridge the gap between new hires and those who were already a part of the team. In most cases, the mentors were your first friends at Digital-Tutors.

My door was always open, but I also recognized that not every new hire wants to come into the founder's office right away. You could always ask your team lead a question, but the mentors would go out of their way to befriend you and offer you another place to ask questions.

There was some job and skillset training, but that first month was mostly about culture training. One of the neatest things we did was the "new hire game." Each new hire had to go to everyone in the company and write down each person's:

- **name**

- **favorite movie**

- **favorite memory at Digital-Tutors**

- **reason for coming to work every day**

Inside of a week, that new hire was exposed to dozens of people recounting the great times they've had and their motivation for getting out of bed in the morning. Not only did they get to meet each person, but they were quickly indoctrinated into "the way we do things around here."

I mentioned earlier that one of the greatest ways to build a sense of belonging is through shared experiences. The new hire game provided the opportunity for the Digital-Tutors tribe to share some of their favorite memories. This was about much more than just sharing something that happened, but without fail it showed the spark of belonging that you, a member of the Digital-Tutors tribe, felt as you relived your favorite memory. There were a number of these stories that became legends in the Digital-Tutors tribe—stories that were passed on from person to person. When a new hire sees that spark, they want to be a part of that experience. They see the meaning this provides, and it's something they want.

The way I saw it, the quicker I could help you make friends with your co-workers, the quicker you'd want to do great work. Our envy-inspiring productivity came from the exponential leverage of our team members working together. The more you became a part of our team, the more exponential value you contributed to the tribe.

Looking back, I also see how this dug the moat even deeper. Where else could you feel that kind of welcome? What other company was going to pour that much care and passion into the lowest guy on the totem pole? After coming on board with Digital-Tutors, I wanted every other job our employees ever had to pale in comparison.

After coming on board with Digital-Tutors, I wanted every other job our employees ever had to pale in comparison.

YOUR TURN!

A first impression can be made only once. As important as they are, most people give a new company some time as they start to learn the ropes. Once you've hired someone, the first thirty days are pivotal to ensuring their success in the tribe. It's make-or-break time.

- **What are you doing to welcome new hires into your tribe?**

- **How are you helping new hires navigate their first month?**

- **What are the legends in your tribe, and how can you communicate them to new hires?**

A first impression can be made only once.

FIRING 11

J eff was a talented designer. He grew up locally, which was a huge plus for me because it meant he had roots in the community and wanted a long-term workplace. I wanted people who were invested in the long-term success of the company.

Jeff loved Digital-Tutors, loved his job, and loved working there. He did great work and made great contributions to the team. He got along with everyone.

I was floored when a couple of people brought his fatal flaw to my attention: he harbored a prejudice. This manifested itself in the subtle ways he acted toward one of his black co-workers. As a teacher for years, I usually clued in on those types of passive-aggressive interactions quickly, but Jeff never acted inappropriately in front of me. When I wasn't around, though, he would "joke" with his co-worker—so much so that other people began to notice a pattern.

When I brought Jeff in to confront the situation, he tried to pass it off as harmless fun: "Aww, he knows I'm just messin' with him!"

I cannot and will not allow any member of my tribe to be belittled, mocked, or the object of someone else's prejudices.

No, Jeff was getting away with subtle racism. His black co-worker didn't think it was funny, his other co-workers didn't think it was funny, and I definitely didn't think it was funny. In a short span of time, he was no longer working at DT.

I cannot and will not allow any member of my tribe to be belittled, mocked, or the object of someone else's prejudices. That's a clear line in the sand because it goes against our core value of respect.

We loved Digital-Tutors. We loved our company, we loved our people, and we loved changing the world. We were on fire and on a mission to set the world on fire. It wasn't by accident. It was by design…and I had to keep it that way.

It was my supreme responsibility to make sure bad guys (and gals) didn't slip past our outer walls and begin to poison us from the inside. I had to make sure that everybody who worked at Digital-Tutors truly belonged there.

FINDING THE RIGHT FIT

No one starts a company with the intention of firing people. It's hard to fire people. It's hard to see your people fail. When they do, though, it's a reflection on you, their leader. Was there something you would have done differently? The teacher in me never wants to give up on someone. Keep teaching or find another way.

In *Good to Great*, Jim Collins said you must have the right people on the bus and in the right seats. Sometimes, that means moving people around until you find the right seat for each of them.

Christian was a great employee who worked hard, had a great attitude, and was a great culture fit. The only problem was with his actual work. I'd hired Christian as an artist, and his artistic ability simply didn't meet our standards. He couldn't keep up.

Originally, Christian did his job well, but as Digital-Tutors grew, he found himself embodying the Peter Principle: he was promoted to his level of incompetence. We gave him more training and tried to develop him beyond his limitations, but it just didn't work.

You can appreciate my dilemma. What could I do with someone like Christian who couldn't do his job but embodied the ethos of Digital-Tutors?

Our leadership team members put their heads together and decided to move him from animation to technical support. Same scenario: commendable spirit, a welcome team member, and awesome outlook…but just as ineffective.

We moved him yet again, this time to production. And do you know what? He blossomed. He was like the back-of-the-room student who finally found a subject he loved and went to the head of the class. He was stellar. Christian used his broad knowledge from experience in almost every facet of our company to develop a production pipeline that vaulted us to levels of production we'd never before been able to accomplish. He became invaluable.

Besides it being a win for him and the management team, it proved to our tribe that we were serious about keeping great people. It showed everybody that we could work on technical aptitude and skillset shortcomings. We truly cared about your attitude. Plus, it was inspiring: it showed that just because you're struggling in your current assignment doesn't mean you can't shine somewhere else. You just need to be sitting in the right seat.

Just because you're struggling in your current assignment doesn't mean you can't shine somewhere else.

THE COST OF LOSING PEOPLE

Up until now, we've talked about the long-term benefit of keeping people motivated. Let's look at the short- and long-term costs of losing people.

The Society for Human Resource Management pegs the direct cost of losing an employee at something like fifty percent of their annual salary. The total cost of losing an employee—that is, the direct costs as well as the indirect costs—can range from ninety percent to even two hundred percent of their annual salary.

Less skilled employees in high turnover jobs (e.g., servers, cashiers, retail salespeople) cost employers less than their highly skilled and/or executive counterparts, but still, the costs are incredible. Let's break those down into three broad categories: financial costs, emotional costs, and opportunity costs.

Some of the direct and indirect financial costs include:

- **severance, accrued time off**

- **wages and salaries of those who have to manage the exit process**

- **wages and salaries of those who have to take up the slack**

- **time and cost to find, vet, and hire a replacement**

- **time and cost of training a replacement**

Opportunity costs are incurred:

- **when team members can't work on projects because they're picking up the slack from the old guy and the new guy**

- **with losing former employees' accumulated domain knowledge**

And the emotional toil incurred:

- **on the owner and other leaders for having to let someone go (whether it's anger, sadness, frustration, or whatever else—it's real)**

- **on the employees as they deal with the absence of a colleague**

- **because of survivor's guilt**

- **when employee, vendors, and customers worry about the impact on the company and their own vested interests**

- **from the fallout of the rumor mill**

All of this can be avoided if you do it right on the front end, rather than trying to "fix" an employee on the back end.

WHEN I HAD TO LET SOMEONE GO

As CEO of Digital-Tutors, firing people was the worst part of my job. I put a lot of fail-safes in place to help ensure firing was a last resort. I'd move someone around, like Christian, in hopes they'd find the right seat on our bus. Or there were the first thirty days with mentors who'd help you fit into the tribe. They would also help identify any red flags that might arise in that time.

Your first thirty days were the dating period. You were still being mentored and getting to know everyone. Firing someone is always painful, but after thirty days the pain is much worse. You're married after thirty days. It's not a break-up anymore—it's a divorce. Letting someone go always tested one of my core values: "We will not tolerate the disrespect of people or property."

No one wants to break up through a text message or phone call. I did my best to offer each tribe member we had to fire the respect they deserved. As hard as it was, I always did it face-to-face. Anger and frustration are symptoms of unfulfilled expectations. Firing someone is an emotional experience that can easily manifest anger and frustration when the person you're letting go has a different set of expectations than you. So, I did my best to make sure those expectations were clear, and offered every opportunity for you to meet them. Maybe it was the teacher in me, always trying to help someone improve. Maybe it was my fear of having to say those words and watch as someone's world fell apart. Maybe it was my fear of my failure as a leader.

If after all those efforts, you were still unwilling or unable to meet expectations, then you had to go. It wasn't fair to the rest of the tribe to expect greatness from them and accept mediocrity from you. As Spock said to Captain Kirk, "The needs of the many outweigh the needs of the few."

By the time you were let go, you knew it was coming…and so did everybody else. We had already had numerous uncomfortable conversations. We had tried to train and retrain you. I had moved you around and attempted to find the right fit. In short, I had done everything I could to help you be the employee you needed to be.

Even though everyone saw the inevitable coming, that doesn't change the fact that this was a person they had gotten to know. They had laughed with us during Thai Thursdays. They weren't strangers. It was painful each and every time. Sometimes the only way to deal with the pain of loss is to let people speak from the heart. So I offered that opportunity. The same day I let someone go, I'd call a meeting with the rest of the company and leave the floor open for anyone else to speak their mind or ask any questions. If anger and frustration are nothing more than unfulfilled expectations, as a business owner, you need to make sure there aren't any unfulfilled expectations. At Digital-Tutors, everyone had the expectation that we were all playing by the rules, a.k.a. our values. When someone wasn't playing by those rules, everyone needed to understand how they were broken.

After sharing the news with the staff, my office door was always open for anyone who may not have wanted to ask their questions in front of the rest of the company. I always encouraged my leadership team to initiate smaller discussions within their teams as well. This opportunity to clear the air also helped manage any mismatched expectations.

YOUR TURN!

Firing someone affects everyone. Stay true to your values. You can mitigate anger and frustration by setting clear expectations up front. Before letting someone go, sit down with them and outline the reasons why they're not fitting into the tribe. If you've outlined the rules of your game, it should be very clear to everyone—including the person you're thinking of letting go—that those values are the standard they need to achieve to work with your tribe.

During many of my coaching sessions, I have leaders who ask what they should do about one of their employees. I never recommend firing as the first recourse. As a leader, it's up to you to exhaust all other options for that member of your tribe. Maybe they don't see where they're failing to align with the tribe's values. To borrow from Jim Collins again, maybe they need a different seat on the bus.

Hopefully, you've started working on a great onboarding process. Now, you need to start working on a solid process for working with challenging employees. Think about one such person on your team. (Nearly everyone has one.) We'll call him "Sam."

- **Why did I originally hire Sam?** What has changed?

- **Which of my core values are being violated?** Why do I feel like firing Sam now?

- **How much of this is the fault of my own failure in leadership and management?**

- **Does Sam exhibit a willingness to change and improve?**

- **Have I clearly communicated to Sam that he isn't meeting expectations?** Does Sam realize there's a problem? If so, does he realize how serious it is? What training can I offer Sam to help him be successful in his current role?

- **What other roles am I trying to fill in my company?** Could Sam grow into one of them?

- **Are there any *new* roles Sam could tackle?**

- **Have I done everything I possibly could to help Sam succeed here?**

- **If I've exhausted every other possibility, why haven't I already fired Sam?** Why am I allowing him to lower the bar for what's acceptable in my company?

TRIBAL LEADERSHIP 12

Doing business in the Digital Age takes more faith than being a business owner in the Industrial Era.

With a factory, you don't have to worry about people stealing your assembly line. If you bought a factory in Asia, short of a political coup, you have a facility in Asia. Your capital investments are tangible and legally yours.

But what about an economy in which your greatest assets can quit any time they damn well please?

People aren't interchangeable. You can't remove one, plug in a replacement, and expect things to run smoothly. You don't have spares sitting on the shelves on which you can fall back if this one has a glitch. So rather than fire someone, we first try to coach them to greatness. Even when they make colossal mistakes.

Like our designer, Steve.

People aren't interchangeable. You can't remove one, plug in a replacement, and expect things to run smoothly.

SEASON'S [GREATINGS]

When Steve joined us, we had about twenty-five people. We put him in charge of ordering our Christmas cards for our annual tradition: everybody got together and made a huge party out of hand-signing all our cards. All one thousand of them.

That's right. Every Christmas, we would send cards to a thousand of our best customers, many of whom had been with us for years. They weren't elaborate cards: just one designed by the team or a picture of the Digital-Tutors crew in Santa Claus hats with a short message inside.

We would form an assembly line. Everybody used a different color pen, signed their name, then passed it down the line. Steve's first year at this event went like any other. Great moods, lots of joking, and that special feeling that only comes with the holidays. Toward the finish, when we could see the end in sight, everyone was winding down and getting ready to go home.

Someone shouted to the head of the table, "Hey, how many do we have left?!"

The reply: "Only ten to go!"

Everybody was excited. We'd had a great time and were ready to wrap it up.

At that exact moment, someone else spoke up: "Hey! Why does the inside of the card read 'Season's Greatings' with an 'A?'" The room went quiet. Then the mad scramble as we all grabbed a card to see for ourselves. Sure enough, as plain as day: *Season's Greatings!*

This, after 25,740 signatures.

Someone said, "Holy shit! We sign a thousand cards and nobody thinks to check this? Who ordered these!?"

You could almost hear Steve's heart hit the floor.

I said, "Okay, okay, how do we fix this?"

One person suggested reordering the cards. Though they wouldn't arrive in time for Christmas, we could wish our customers a Happy New Year's. I didn't like it, though. We always sent out Christmas cards. That's just what Digital-Tutors did.

Then, someone else had a great idea: why not cut the card in half along the fold, throw away the message, and just sign the back of the photograph? Brilliant.

Everybody ran to get paper cutters and x-acto knives and got to work. We cut one thousand cards. Then Tina and Lisa, who we all agreed had the best handwriting, sat at the front of the assembly line and wrote "Season's Greetings" on each card. Then they passed the card down the line where we went through the whole process again.

When we were done and everyone was packing up to go home, I pulled Steve aside. He was as scared as shit. You could see the "I am so fired" in his eyes.

I put my arm around him and said, "Hey buddy, tell me what you learned from this."

He swallowed hard and said, "We're never going to have anything misspelled again."

I said, "Thank you. I know you won't."

He nodded, and the relief that he wasn't getting fired showed.

From then on, Steve was our go-to guy on anything like that. He created a pre-flight and post-flight checklist so we had a process in place to make sure nothing like that ever happened again.

But you know what I think I'm most proud of?

No one screamed and blamed Steve. They kept their heads, worked on the problem, and even joked about it for days afterward. While they were frustrated, they didn't take it out on Steve. They had made mistakes before and the team took up the slack. They paid it forward by pitching in to cover for Steve's mistake.

That is how a true tribe works.

EOM MEETINGS

In the "Affirmation" chapter, I touched on the only all-staff meeting we had at Digital-Tutors. We dubbed the meeting the EOM: end of month. I already talked about the first sixty minutes of the meeting with the values stories and their importance in providing B.A.M. to the tribe.

But what about the second half of the meeting?

After values stories were finished, I'd hand the meeting over to each team lead to have them share an update with the company. To force this to be concise and to keep from eating up everyone's time, I'd tell the team leads ahead of time to limit their information to four presentation slides. Each month, each team would share the four most important things that everybody needed to know. As we grew, we started using the Entrepreneurial Operating System (EOS), so this was the chance for each team lead to share their "rocks" or priorities with the company and if they weren't on track, to say why.

Once all the teams had given their updates, I'd share important dates and financials. The important dates could be upcoming holidays, charity events, or new hire start dates. We were an "open book" company and I'd share any relevant company financials at the meeting. We didn't go over every line item, but I shared the core numbers. Where were we? Winning? Losing? By how much? This provided a bigger picture for where we were compared to where we wanted to be. Offering transparency into our financials went a long way to helping alleviate unfulfilled expectations. Our monetary goal was clear to everyone in the company and each month everyone knew how near or far we were from hitting it.

Last, but not least, our EOM would wrap up with something that was the most valuable part of the meeting for me: takeaways. We'd go around the room and every person would share the biggest thing they were taking away from the meeting.

It gave me insight into each person. I could measure what I thought the takeaway was against what each individual thought. If they missed the big idea, it meant something was off; there was a disconnect somewhere. At the end of the day, it's all about whether or not the message you're trying to send is the one being received.

OFFICE HOURS

When I was a professor, I had office hours. When I became CEO, I kept the practice. The difference was that as a CEO, I got to have my office hours at a bar. It was a set time to visit with me outside the office walls.

Everybody knew that on Mondays from six to eight o'clock, you could find me at McNellie's Pub, right down the street from the office. Anybody was welcome, from the receptionist to the

COO, but without any pressure. Show up or not; it was completely up to you.

It was great. Sometimes one person would show up for drinks and we'd just talk about our families, video games, new movies, or whatever. Sometimes a big group would show up, so we'd grab a table and relive a rock star road trip. Sometimes no one came and I enjoyed a drink and a book by myself. Regardless, I was there. McNellie's Mondays became an institution at Digital-Tutors.

Here's the beauty of this Monday ritual: it was like having an open-door policy, but at an off-site, low-key environment. When it was one-on-one, sometimes our conversations turned into coaching, where I could help somebody through something with which they were struggling. Two colleagues might break off from the big group and hash out something privately, maybe work-related or maybe a personal misunderstanding. Sometimes, I'd ask somebody for a minute and have a heart-to-heart with them about an issue where they needed to pick it up.

Instead of our home away from home, McNellie's became our work away from work. It wasn't mandatory. People dropped in or left as they wanted to. I didn't always drink. Many times, I just had a club soda. Drinks weren't on me. We treated it just as if we were all equal co-workers. Sometimes I would pick up the tab and the other person would say, "Oh, thanks, Piyush. I've got the next round!" Or I'd see someone slipping the bartender their credit card and I'd say, "Drinks on you today? Thank you! I'll get us next time."

Mind you, there were five other bars as near as McNellie's. But that was *our* bar. If there was a wait, I waited. Come what may, Piyush was going to be at McNellie's on Monday at six. Always. Some of

Annual reviews never made sense to me.

our best ideas came from the wild ideas we threw out. Some relationships got repaired. Some deep friendships were made.

What I created was a non-threatening, relaxed place that was always available—for camaraderie, for intimate chats, for frank discussions, for a fun hangout, for a stress reliever, or for whatever our team needed.

Where's your McNellie's?

CONSTANT COACHING

Annual reviews never made sense to me. They're a holdover from the Industrial Era, when things moved so slowly that assessing someone's performance over a year was enough. But we don't live in the 1850s or even the 1950s. We've been in the new millennium for a while now. It's time we started acting like it.

Business moves at a fast pace, especially in tech. So by the time a performance review happens, the relevant feedback is already months out of date. More importantly, people shouldn't have to wait months for their boss to acknowledge a job well done. When someone did something great at Digital-Tutors, they knew it. When someone did something that needed coaching, we gave it.

Feedback, praise, and communication constantly happened in real time at our offices: up and down, peer-to-peer, friend-to-friend, intra-team, inter-team, and in every other imaginable way. We were a tight-knit crew by design. Our 3 Happies, McNellie's Mondays, and our monthly meetings all set the tone that communication—positive or otherwise—was okay, encouraged, and expected.

Perhaps one of the best examples of this was with our course release schedule. For years, we released new training courses on a month-to-month basis. Each release included a batch of twenty or so courses and was a huge undertaking for everyone in the company. Every team was involved.

While this worked for a time, teams were so exhausted after meeting each monthly release deadline that our ability to fix current features or add new ones was severely diminished. Simultaneously, as online video training became more popular, I knew we needed to overhaul monthly releases. In an internet-driven world, releasing something new once a month wasn't going to take us to where we wanted to go.

Constant coaching and communication was key to being able to embrace positive change. As with most things, there wasn't an overnight solution. With my tribe's goal being clear, we could set projects and tasks to continually refine and improve our processes to accomplish the goal.

Within two years, we went from a monthly release of about twenty courses to releasing one to three courses a day. At the same time, the releases went from a major project that nearly every team had a hand in to something one employee could manage.

We did away with the need for annual reviews because we were constantly analyzing, constantly checking in, and constantly improving.

YOUR TURN!

Benjamin Franklin started each morning by asking himself the question, "What good shall I do this day?" Whether through setting up rituals for regular coaching or by taking advantage of opportunities when they arise, such as Steve's "Season's Greatings" mistake, you'll have to work to make each day better than the last. Set up a ritual to help you start each day with the purpose of helping or coaching at least one person in your tribe. Here are a few questions you can ask yourself every morning to get started:

- **Whom will I help be a better leader today?**

- **Whom will I coach through a new solution to a difficult challenge today?**

- **Whom will I help with better communication today?**

Each day, make a concerted effort to help someone else.

HAVING "THOSE" CONVERSATIONS 13

In every company (heck, in every family), you must have "those" conversations from time to time. You know what I'm talking about.

The kind of talk where your stomach drops, your hands get clammy, and you're nervous because you don't know how it's going to go. This goes for both sides: the person who needs to say it and the one who needs to hear it. I'm a nice guy (or so they tell me); I don't like having "those" conversations. But as a business owner, an employer, and a leader, I need to have those kinds of talks.

The trouble is that, as the boss, I could never just have normal conversations. One time, I invited Marcus to lunch. I could tell he was wary. We sat down, ordered our food, and started talking about NBA basketball. Or, at least, I did; he was quiet the whole time. When we finished, I stood to leave. Marcus said, "That's it?"

I was confused. "Is what it?"

"That's...that's all? I thought...I thought, I don't know, I thought I was getting fired."

Shocked, I sat back down. "Why in the world would you think you were fired? You're doing a great job! We love you."

He said, "Well, I mean, when the boss takes you out to lunch—I don't know, you just assume the worst."

That was my clue. Marcus had extensive experience at other companies before coming to Digital-Tutors, so it's possible he'd been fired, or at least given bad news, over lunch by the boss. I had never set the expectations for when a difficult conversation would take place, so he assumed they could happen at any time.

I didn't want people to get freaked out every time I invited them to lunch or to a meeting in my office, so I had to create a system or process that would set clear expectations up front. I created the "Principal's Office": a small conference room dedicated solely to "uncomfortable conversations," as we called them. It was the only place any of us could have "those" kinds of talks. If you weren't meeting in there, you knew everything was alright. If you *were* meeting in there, you at least knew to prepare yourself. It was for anybody, not just me. If you needed to hash something out with your team leader or a peer, the two of you went in, dealt with it, and then came to a resolution. Once we had the Principal's Office, you never had to worry about being blindsided. If an uncomfortable conversation was going to happen, it was going to happen in there. By default, everywhere else was a safe zone. No worries about your team lead ambushing you at dinner or in the hallway. No fears that you'd get an email delivering the bad news. No wondering whether or not the "coaching" that the boss scheduled with you the following day was just a disguised chewing out. Nothing like that. A conversation in any other place always meant that you were just trying to solve a problem.

Create a principals office for "uncomfortable conversations."

A CONSTRUCTIVE UNCOMFORTABLE CONVERSATION

You can't avoid conflict.

That's a fact of business. If you put two people together, they will, at some point, have a problem with each other. That happens even in the best of environments and the happiest of marriages. It's inevitable.

But how do you handle the conflict? That tells the tale.

If your employee promises to have a task completed by Wednesday and you still don't have it by Friday, what do you do? Storm into their workspace, demanding they get it done? Berate them for being incompetent? Assume they're lazy and start talking behind their back?

Two problems with that approach. For one, it doesn't solve the problem. Two—and this is the kicker—it spawns a whole new host of troubles. When you shift the focus from the problem to the person, you attack them personally. Think back. Can you still hear former teachers, relatives, or classmates taunting you with jabs or insults? You may not even remember why they said the hurtful thing they did, but you can still remember the pain. When you do that in a business setting, you're doing the same thing. Now, not only is the problem not solved, but you've hurt your employee.

Depending on their personality, they may hold a grudge, sabotage future work, go home and break down, ratchet down their effort, or resent you.

Attacking the person never produces a positive result.

Both inside the Principal's Office and elsewhere, we used a model of conflict resolution called G.R.O.W.:

- **Goals**
- **Reality**
- **Options**
- **What by when?**

Sometimes uncomfortable conversations are one-on-one conversations and sometimes they need to happen with multiple people. Here's how an actual G.R.O.W. meeting transpired at DT with Kevin, Christian, Glenn, Pete, and Darrin. This was an unusually large group so we had to pull in a few extra chairs, but after everyone filed into the Principal's Office, I began:

"Hey guys, we need to have an uncomfortable conversation."

I could tell by the looks on their faces that only about half of the group knew what this was about. I explained the situation, "A customer called this morning. She was upset after watching one of our new Photoshop courses that just came out. She said she could barely understand what was being said and after watching it, I agree—we must do better. Everyone in this room had a hand in creating that course from start to finish."

No one said anything, so I continued.

"Let's figure out how to resolve this and make sure it doesn't happen again in the future."

I got up and went to the white board and wrote the letters **G.R.O.W.** down the left side of the board. Next to the **G**, I wrote the goal: "We produce high-quality video content with clear audio and video."

Then I wrote the reality I had just explained next to **R**: "The new Photoshop course was released and had multiple videos with audio that was barely audible."

I turned around, "What are our options?"

After a moment, Darrin broke the silence.

"I'm sorry guys," she said. "I should've caught that."

"We're all responsible," Christian said. "I remember that course. We had a lot of errors and it took a long time to get it from the author. I thought it wasn't great, but I knew it'd take even longer to get him to re-record stuff, so I let it go through anyway."

"What's done is done," I moved the conversation along, "Talk to me about what options we can do to move forward."

I could see the gears start turning as everyone focused on solving the problem. Within a few moments, this went from an uncomfortable conversation about dropping the ball on one course to a chance to solve a problem and improve the quality of all our courses. Everyone was throwing out ideas. I wrote down the options as the team thought of them. After fifteen minutes, the ideas started to slow down. We had five options on the board:

- **Have the author re-record the problem videos in this course**

- **Add more quality control steps**

- **Improve our pipeline to be able to identify these issues**

- **Make it more transparent to everyone involved when a course is getting off track or could be prone to errors**

- **Communicate better between teams**

"Great," I said, looking at the list of options. "Now what will we do, and by when?"

Everyone started throwing out action items. Kevin would call the author and ask him to re-record as soon as he got out of the meeting. Glenn would work with the dev team next sprint to build a long-term solution for our internal tools to clearly identify a course as being error-prone. In the interim, Christian would notify Pete in quality assurance about which videos needed a lot of edits so Pete would know to check those videos more closely. Finally, by the end of the week, Darrin would build a process for everyone working on our backend software so each course had someone accountable for it and communication could be clearer across the teams.

The whole meeting took about half an hour, and not only was the course updated within a week, but we had new processes in place to keep similar issues from happening in the future.

Now imagine if I'd barged in there with guns blazing: "You don't know how to do your shit! Why can't you just do what you're supposed to!?" Immediately, everyone would be on the defensive, we wouldn't get nearly as much resolved, and the meeting itself probably would've taken twice as long.

This is important: as the boss, I didn't give the team an ultimatum. I laid out the parameters—the business reality—and then let them come up with a solution that worked within that. That way, my team owned the solution and committed themselves to living up to the expectation they had set.

Here's the other important piece: by focusing on the reality and the solution, we took the emotional element out of the equation. The conflict didn't turn into a trial of their sins and personal shortcomings. We looked at where we were, where we wanted to be, and then charted a course to get from Point A to Point B.

Once I began following this system, team leaders began using it with their teams. Eventually even co-workers used it to solve problems between each other. The transformation fascinated me: conversations that could have easily resulted in people holding grudges for days—if not years—went off without a hitch. People walked into the Principal's Office and walked out laughing.

It was just another one of those things that made our tribe magical.

YOUR TURN!

When a fire breaks out, what do you do? Don't wait until you see the flames to figure it out. Safety experts always suggest having a plan in place, knowing your fire escape routes, and practicing this plan with everyone. That way, everyone will know what to do when an emergency occurs.

Although you never know when you'll need to have an uncomfortable conversation, try to keep in mind that a) you *will* have to have to them eventually, and b) you'll be better off if you're prepared for them.

Set up times to introduce the G.R.O.W. model with everyone. Try keeping the size of the meeting small, with no more than eight people. This goes a long way to ensuring everyone is practicing listening as an act of affirmation while you're explaining the concepts. It also helps when you need to answer questions people may have.

**My team owned
the solution and
committed themselves
to living up to the
expectation they
had set.**

The key takeaways for your team are:

- **An understanding of what each letter in G.R.O.W. means**
  - **Goals**
  - **Reality**
  - **Options**
  - **What by when?**

- **The ability to construct a conversation around the G.R.O.W. model**

- **Bonus: the ability (and confidence) for people to lead their own G.R.O.W. meeting**

For the last two takeaways, your team needs to be able to apply the G.R.O.W. model to actual situations in your company. So, in your meeting, run through some sample everyday scenarios. It's better if they're not uncomfortable situations yet, as this can help your team recognize how G.R.O.W. is all about everyone being on the same page about mismatched expectations. And, as we learned in earlier chapters, this helps mitigate anger and frustration.

G.R.O.W. is about everyone being on the same page versus about mismatched expectations.

TEAMWORK BY DESIGN 14

Although Lisa was technically co-owner of Digital-Tutors, she left most of the company leadership up to me. She was happy to take care of the payroll and human resource duties. But Lisa's most important contribution to our company might have been her role as the unofficial "office mom." We put her degree in Family Relations and Child Development to good use.

When someone would come in feeling under the weather, Lisa would take one look at them and send them home: "You're too sick to be working. Go home, get some rest, and eat plenty of chicken noodle soup."

Sometimes, people would come in and just seem…off. Lisa would notice and ask, "Hey, is everything okay?" Sometimes, just that question might result in tears. Lisa would say, "Alright. Come in. Let's hear about it."

Heartache. Heartbreak. Family trouble. Children trouble. Financial issues. Anxiety issues. She heard it all. With Lisa, you always knew she would listen. You knew she cared. By the time you were finished, the two of you might not have solved anything, but at least you felt better for being able to talk to someone. And often, that's all her tribe needed: just to have someone hear them out and know they weren't alone.

Now, let's switch gears and talk about how much that cost. While ninety percent of Lisa's duties were HR- and payroll-related, she was still part of the leadership team and weighed in on major decisions. Her time and attention were valuable. When she was being the office mom, not only was I paying their time, but their productivity suffered. And believe me, these talks could go on at length.

Of course, it wasn't all bad. People wanted to share their successes, too: their new date, what their cute kid had done lately, a personal milestone they'd achieved. Either way, Lisa's office was a revolving door. Yes, it definitely cut into profit and productivity in the short term.

But what a great investment!

I know that if you're having relationship issues, if your marriage is on the rocks, or whatever it is, you're more worried about your personal problems than you are about my business (basic Maslow's hierarchy, right?). You may have shown up to the office physically, but mentally you're still rehashing a fight at the house or arguing with your child on the phone. You showed up, but you're not here.

Having an office mom let our team members work off some steam or feel happy about sharing something great. It let them get it—whatever "it" was—out of their system. It helps to talk. It stops that endless playback loop of "I can't believe they said that…" or the infinite what-if scenarios.

To be frank, Lisa helped you get your shit together so you could get shit done.

Getting it out of your head let you calm down, feel some sense of hope, and then let you be clearheaded so you could get to work. I'd rather have you at work for four hours at ninety-percent capacity than for you to work for eight hours at thirty-percent capacity.

When you're at peace in your personal life, you'll get more done in your professional life and be a better team member. The whole tribe wins and gets more done.

WALKING DOWN MAIN STREET

Not everybody drinks coffee. Not everybody uses the printer on a regular basis. Not everybody takes lunch at the same time. But you know what?

Everybody goes to the bathroom.

Just a fact of life. At some point in the day, you have to go…and one of the smartest decisions I ever made was to design our new offices around the bathrooms.

Yes, we had an impressive lobby and creative workspaces, but by centralizing the bathrooms, everybody had to go through "main street" to get to them.

It virtually guaranteed that everybody in the office was going to see everybody else at some point during the week. This was especially important for teams that didn't work directly with each other. They might not have any other excuse to interact with each other. But when they saw each other coming and going, they might have an impromptu conversation or at least exchange a friendly hello, reinforcing the relationship there.

It's also where we hung up our Happies to learn something about co-workers we didn't know before: "Oh, you went kayaking this

When you're at peace in your personal life, you'll get more done in your professional life and be a better team member. The whole tribe wins and gets more done.

weekend? I love camping. Maybe we should organize a small camping trip with some others in the office."

As the company grew and had to add on more space, the new area we took over included another set of bathrooms. Overnight, we lost our Main Street; a third of our tribe didn't use the same area anymore. While there were still plenty of other ways we reinforced our tribal connections, I could feel the change. If I had it to do over again, I'd have redesigned the new space around the bathrooms.

HOW TO GET SHIT DONE

Nobody works forty hours a week.

You may be at work for forty hours, but that's not actually the amount of time spent on productivity. You've got to go to the bathroom (as we just discussed), you have meetings, you have emails and calls to return, you need to stretch your legs, you have conversations in the kitchen, you get counseling from the office mom—whatever it is, it's less than forty.

I just acknowledged the truth of it.

At Digital-Tutors, we roughly followed a process common among software developers called "agile." I say "roughly" because we had no hesitation improving any process to work for our needs. For a long time, we went old school: yellow Post-It notes on a whiteboard. We'd draw up three columns on the whiteboard: "To-Do," "In Progress," and "Done." We'd always kick off our weekly team meetings, called "sprints" in agile terms, by reviewing the work done since the last time we met. In these retrospectives, we'd go around as a team and discuss what went well in the past week and what we could've done better. As a team, we'd celebrate our wins, no matter how small, and also keep the need for constant improvement at the forefront.

Ideally, every Post-It would be hanging under the "Done" column on the whiteboard when we met to add more to the board. If something wasn't "Done," we'd have a team discussion around the unfinished projects. An unfinished project isn't always an uncomfortable conversation, but I'd often revert to a quick G.R.O.W.-inspired discussion to find out why something didn't get completed. What did we want to get done with the ticket (reiterate the goal)? Where were we on it (the current reality)? How much work was left (the options)? Was it still something we wanted to get done (what, by when)? Sometimes what was a priority last week wasn't a priority this week.

After reviewing any incomplete projects, we'd shift our focus to the future. "Okay, out of the forty hours you're physically here, let's estimate thirty hours are available for getting shit done."

If there were five people in the room, that meant 150 man-hours for tasks. We would look at our five-year goals, yearly goals, quarterly goals, and monthly goals, then break down any tasks this team needed to accomplish in the next week to reach every milestone (a spin on Gino Wickman's Traction system).

Each person on the team came to the sprint prepared with several projects in their backlog—an agile term for a to-do list of projects. Then we'd go around the room one at a time and agree on the work each person would get done.

Christina might go first one week and list the first project she wanted to add to the whiteboard, say, reprocessing all the images for the newsletter. She'd give a brief rundown of the project, why she thought it was important to it get done this week, and say, "I can get that done in a day." Then we'd have a quick discussion to determine if it was something we needed to get done that week and if we wanted to allocate a day's worth of Christina's time to the project.

After we all agreed to Christina's project, she'd jot down "1 day" with the project's name and put it in the "To-Do" column on the whiteboard before moving on to her next project. One by one, each member of the team would go through their projects for the next week. At the end of the meeting, we'd review what everyone had on the board one last time and then get back to work.

The Post-Its and whiteboard were just tools. As the company grew, we replicated our physical whiteboard system using online tools everyone could access from anywhere. But the concept of giving a time estimate was important. That's how we knew we'd get the right amount of work done without putting too little or too much on anyone's plate.

It might take Christina a day every few months to reprocess the images for the newsletter. But someone, say Kevin, might be able to spend a day scripting a tool Christina could use to reprocess the images in an hour. If that were the case, we'd almost always opt for building a tool or designing a workflow that could automate the process. That'd free up more of Christina's time to let her focus on creative work, like exploring new design ideas for the newsletter. It also revealed who was great at what. If designing new wireframes for the site consistently took Christina three hours but took Lucas only one, obviously that's a strength for Lucas. We know who's good at what. It's a quantifiable fact: Lucas always delivers wireframes faster than Christina. It's a great self-inventory but also a great management inventory: the leader knows what skillsets are in people's toolkit.

But you know what? Estimates are never perfect. No matter how

You were responsible for your own success, but everyone was also responsible for the team's success.

many times you try to estimate projects, there will always be times when the estimates are off. You need to be okay with that.

At Digital-Tutors, if you overestimated how much time a task would take and you finished everything you had on the board early, our tribe mentality meant you'd check with the rest of the team first to see if you could help them with their projects for the sprint. If not, you'd communicate with your team lead and pull a new project from your backlog—in other words, get a head start on something you planned to do the following week.

Yes, you were responsible for your own success, but everyone was also responsible for the team's success. If Lucas came to next week's sprint and hadn't gotten everything done, it wasn't just Lucas who'd came up short; it was the team. If the team didn't meet its weekly goals, how could the team meet its monthly, quarterly, and yearly goals?

It was also important to have a discussion in our retrospective to figure out why Lucas' estimates weren't correct. At the beginning of the sprint, Lucas thought he could get everything done. But he didn't. What happened? How did reality differ from our goal? This helped us improve our future estimates. The more time we'd spend on estimating, the more we improved at estimating and the fewer projects were left incomplete at the end of a sprint.

YOUR TURN!

How do you know if you're winning or losing? For most business owners, an oversimplified answer would be the profit and loss statement. How much money do you have coming in against how much is being spent? Now answer this question: what is one of your largest expenses? While there are always exceptions, I'd be willing to bet payroll is one of—if not the most—expensive costs in your company. Your tribe's time is vital to its success. So how do you know if your people are bringing more to the table than they cost?

One of the easiest ways to know if you're winning or losing with your tribe's efforts is to start having them estimate their work hours. Before I continue, let me be very clear: I am not advocating the blanket use of timesheets. While they may have a place in some industries, they don't fit everywhere. We didn't use them at Digital-Tutors.

Instead, what I'm referring to is a simple conversation about whether or not the time your tribe is spending on projects fulfills expectations. It's what we saw Christina do earlier in this chapter when she estimated her project would take one day. You don't have to switch to an in-depth agile development workflow with sprints and retrospectives, but try dedicating the next thirty days to this formula:

- **Have the person who's accountable for a project estimate how long they think it'll take before it begins.** Jot this down somewhere you can refer back to later.

- **When the project is done, do a simple comparison.** If there's a discrepancy, have a conversation around that.

Initially, it may seem like you're trying to micromanage, but you can avoid that by setting expectations up front. You're not trying to find out who works the fastest. You're trying to find out if Christina's goal of spending one day on a project matches the reality. If not, it's up to you to find out why. Did she have roadblocks? As a leader, your job is to clear those. Did someone ask her to work on a different project? Legitimate emergency projects can pop up, but the decision to shift from one project to another should be a conscious one. If it's not, there will be unfulfilled expectations that can lead to anger and frustration.

These conversations are a time for you to practice listening as an act of affirmation. Listen to your tribe and they'll tell you what's keeping them from getting stuff done. Then it's your job to help them overcome those obstacles.

LEADERS GO LAST 15

Plenty of small business and entrepreneurship advice says you should pay yourself first. I get it. If the owner isn't making any money, then their family starves, right? Eventually, the owner has to close their doors and find a job, which means all of their employees lose their jobs.

I've been there. I can't tell you how many months Lisa and I went without a paycheck. She'd look at me and ask, "Piyush, how long can we sustain this?"

I'd say, "However long it takes."

She'd point out that we were paying everybody but ourselves.

"I know, Lisa, I know. But we can't *not* pay them. We employ them. As the owners, we promised not only to pay them, but to pay them on time. We're taking the risk that Digital-Tutors might fail and drag us down financially or take off and make a lot of money—but that's our problem. We can't make it their problem, too."

An employee comes to work, implicitly promising me that they'll get their work done. The trade is that, when payroll time comes, they'll get paid for services rendered. It's that simple.

If I start screwing around with their paycheck, I'm breaking my promise to them. I'm damaging our relationship. If I don't deliver on my commitment to them, why should they deliver on their commitment to me? If their personal welfare isn't a priority to me, why should the welfare of my business be a priority to them?

I was committed to keeping my promise. When I was fifteen years old, I set a goal that when I turned thirty, I'd buy a Corvette. It took me the full fifteen years, but I worked hard, and got one. A gorgeous orange Corvette, actually. I don't indulge in many luxuries, but cars are my vice. At that time, though, that Corvette was my first real indulgence. I loved it.

About six months later we were staring down the barrel at payroll Friday with $500 in the bank. I'm not joking. The only thing I could think of was to sell my car. Since I had to sell it fast, I took out an ad on Autotrader.com. I took pictures and filled out all the details, then posted it online. Immediately, I had a bite. The next day, a guy was coming out to look at it.

A friend asked me that evening, "Are you really willing to sell your car for these people? You're sure?"

I said, "Yeah. I'm willing to do whatever it takes. I can't miss payroll. That's breaking a promise. Once I break that trust, I'll never regain it."

The next day, a miracle happened: a big order was called in. I was on the phone with them and said, "Look, if you'll pay today, we'll give you a 10% discount." The purchaser thought that sounded great and wired the money. We made payroll that Friday, I took my car off Autotrader, and no one was ever the wiser. I kept my promise to my people.

I always took care of my tribe and they always took care of me.

LEAD WITH PANCAKES

One Friday morning, we did a pancake breakfast at the office. That is, *I* did a pancake breakfast. I bought the groceries, brought the equipment, set everything up, and had batter sizzling on the griddle when the first person showed up to work. We all had a great time, my employees loved it, the office smelled amazing, and the pancakes were perfect (or so they told me).

We didn't stop at pancakes. Once a year, we'd also host a family picnic. Everybody brought their kids, spouses, significant others, or whomever, and played in the park the whole day. I donned my "kiss the cook" apron and barbecued for everybody. Again, we all had a great time and felt like the family we were. I always thought it was important that my employees see me in settings where I was serving them, literally and figuratively. Yes, I was the founder, owner, and CEO. Kind of hard to forget that fact. But I wanted some tangible way to demonstrate that taking care of my tribe was my job; taking care of the customer was theirs. They needed to see that our relationship wasn't a one-way street.

Sure, I could have ordered takeout instead of cooking it myself. Yes, I could have had breakfast catered with Starbucks pastries. But me buying something isn't nearly as powerful as me doing something.

SINCERE GENEROSITY

When we sold Digital-Tutors, we wanted to make a final lasting impact to our employees.

Lisa and I believe in the practice of giving back. In this instance, we decided to give to our employees. We went back to the office and divided $4.5 million among our thirty-two employees based on time spent working with us, with some extra bonuses for the leadership team.

Some of those folks walked in that morning thinking it was just a regular day, and by the end of the day, they'd paid off their mortgages. It was phenomenal. Literally, life-changing.

Why?

Why would Lisa and I willingly—happily—fork over $4.5 million dollars? It certainly wasn't for the tax incentives. We didn't get a pat on the back from Uncle Sam for employee bonuses. We'd have gotten at least a small break for giving it to our church or another nonprofit organization. We didn't do it because we were behind on other promised bonuses. We didn't do it because they expected it of us.

We did it because we knew that without their commitment and dedication, we wouldn't have had a company of tremendous value to a buyer in the first place. Our people are what made Digital-Tutors the company it was.

We did it because we practiced affirmation—even when we weren't leaders anymore.

YOUR TURN!

In the "Onboarding" chapter, I mentioned how I'd give every new hire one of my favorite books, *Leaders Eat Last* by Simon Sinek. I won't try to re-invent the wheel here: make Simon's book next on your list to read.

As you read it, I want you to come up with three ways to practice generosity:

1. **As a leader: find a way to demonstrate service to your employees.** Cook, if you like to cook. Be a bartender if you like to mix drinks. That worked for me. Find something that works for you. Whatever it is, it must be a demonstrable action—something you do.

2. **As a family member: find a way to serve your closest loved ones on a regular basis.** If you have a spouse or partner, do something they would love. (Go read *The 5 Love Languages* by Gary Chapman for ideas.)

3. **As a giver: find a worthy cause and donate your time and money.** I am involved with Infant Crisis Services, which provides life sustaining food, diapers, and clothing for babies and toddlers in times of crisis. Find something to help you remember that life is a lot bigger than you, but also that other people out there need your help.

WHEN YOU'RE A SHITTY LEADER 16

My friend Brandon owns a specialty roofing company in Texas. His business grosses almost $5 million a year. At one point, his was perhaps the best company in town.

Today, Brandon hates going to work. He hates his employees, he hates selling, and he hates helping. He doesn't have a shoddy business; things still get done and he still grosses seven figures a year. But these days, Brandon realizes that it has to be about more than just the money. Or, about more than just putting another roof on a house. It has to be about more than just…well, just having more.

I'd sit and listen to him bitch and moan: "My people won't get their shit done. Why can't they just do it right? I can't even trust them to do their own damn job. I have to do it all!"

But I've watched him interact with his employees: "No, no, no! You're not doing it right! Just—here, let me show you how to do it."

It has to be about more than just having more.

No wonder they don't have much initiative. I wouldn't either if I knew that, no matter what I did, the boss was just going to come behind me and redo it, and chew me out while he did so.

Belonging? Zip.

In Brandon's mind, it's him against the lazy slackers. For Brandon, employees are a necessary evil. There's no sense of being part of something for his employees. To them, he's just a paycheck—and a boot in the ass.

Affirmation? Zero.

In fact, just the opposite. Instead of making his employees feel fulfilled, he belittles them and shreds their contributions to pieces.

Meaning? Zilch.

They don't even belong to Brandon's tribe, much less find meaning in it. You can find meaning in the most mundane jobs—if you want to. Specialty roofing may not be sexy, but it's an important part of modern life. It ranks right up there with food and water on mankind's basic needs. A roof protects people and virtually all their worldly possessions.

But does Brandon try to instill a sense of meaning and purpose in his company? Absolutely not. It's easier to pretend that the problem lies in the employees instead of looking at the man in the mirror.

KEEP DIGGING UNTIL YOU FIND THE PROBLEM

When clients come to me for help or coaching, they want me to fix the problem: sales are down, customer complaints are up, and costs are through the roof.

When I look at their business, products, services, and market, I usually see different things they should fix right off the bat. The product doesn't align with the targeted demographic. There's an execution problem. There's a missed opportunity in packaging services together.

But those are incremental fixes. They don't drive down to the heart of the problem: I've got to find what you really want from your business.

It can't just be "more money."

You can't lead your tribe and love your work just around the idea of making more money. Money is the byproduct of having a community that has a sense of purpose and accomplishes something for the greater good. Your profits help you keep score of how well you're doing, but they are only one indicator of success (albeit an incredibly important one). So, when I start mentoring someone, the first thing I want to know is, "What's important to you?" I need to understand what you stand for, why you do what you do, and what you believe.

By what values do you live? For what are willing to stand? For what aren't you willing to stand? You've got to get honest with yourself and clear about what makes you tick before you can lead anybody else.

If you're leading in one direction, but your heart's not in it, you won't get very far. Not in any kind of meaningful way that makes life worth living. I guess for Brandon, the problem is that his heart's not in it. He hates his employees, he hates his customers, he hates his store, and he's generally miserable.

Why the hell would you want to live like that?

You can't lead your tribe and love your work just around the idea of making more money.

GO FIND HELP

I have an easygoing friend who's the CEO at a family-owned auto parts store. One day, Tom had an argument with one of his kids right before dropping them off at school. When he got to work, he was still stewing. He came in—obviously mad—went straight to his office, closed the door, and stayed in there until he could cool off.

By the time he emerged, the store was rife with rumors. Was there a problem? Were people about to get laid off? What was going on? People had completely flipped out because his behavior was so out of character. Just a little bickering with his kid resulted in shock waves throughout the company.

As the owner of a company, every day is a performance. I don't mean that you should put on a show. I am always the same person, regardless of where you find me. At the office, at McNellie's, at home, at the grocery store—no matter where you meet me, I am the same person.

But that meant every day, I had people from all directions watching me. My employees, my executive team, my customers, and my suppliers were all connected to me because we had a business relationship.

The implicit question every human asks is, "What's in it for me?"

Yes, I believe many—maybe even most—of those people genuinely care about me as a human being. But because we're connected by business, I need to remain aware that our relationship has a commercial aspect to it.

Imagine telling your COO or one of your investors, "You know, I've been feeling kind of depressed lately. I don't know what's going on." While your COO may try to cheer you up, they might also have a bell sounding off in the back of their head, telling them it's time to update their résumé. There were only a few people in my organization (besides Lisa, of course) with whom I could completely let go and not worry about how things sounded; I didn't have to be slightly guarded to make sure I didn't let something slip. As the owner, you're constantly weighing your words to make sure they don't adversely affect the people around you.

That's why Entrepreneurs' Organization (EO) was such a godsend. It's not a networking group; it's a peer-to-peer support group. My fellow EOers had no vested interest in my business decisions. I could talk frankly about issues without worrying about how the message was being received and interpreted.

It is lonely at the top...I wouldn't be who I am today without the sage experience shared by my EO forum mates.

YOUR TURN!

If you want your company to grow...well, *you* have to grow. If you want work to be a great workplace...you have to be a great person to be around. If you want your business to be awesome... you have to be awesome. Your takeaway from this chapter is to find the help you need. Here are a few ideas to get you started:

- **Books: you should always be reading a book.**

- **Continuing education: keep an eye out and take advantage of new learning opportunities.** This could be anything from conferences to finding a mentor with whom to bounce off ideas.

- **Peer groups: for me, it was joining the Entrepreneurs' Organization.**

GO FORTH AND LEAD A TRIBE

17

Values mean nothing if you don't practice them. Your mission and vision statements mean nothing if they don't guide you and your tribe. Plastering them on the walls doesn't magically infuse them into your company's culture.

You'll notice I haven't said anything about Digital-Tutors' mission statement or our company vision. Author Simon Sinek says to begin with "the golden circle" and start with *why*. Why do you what to do what you are doing? Why does your company exist? Why is this important?

At the risk of sounding existential: why are you here?

Whatever the answer, that's your why. How you achieve that is your mission. As circumstances change and your company grows and matures, your mission will necessarily change. But your vision, if you have clarity, should stay the same.

Digital-Tutors wasn't in business to make tutorials. That's *what* we did, and everyone in the tribe was passionate about what we did, but that's not the *why* behind what we did. At Digital-Tutors, our mission was: *Teaching the people who make movies and games.* As we grew, what we did changed. We switched from CDs to an online subscription. We added tutorials for other industries, including web design and architecture. Our mission changed.

The *why* never did.

You wouldn't have found that *why* on a wall in our offices. You wouldn't have found it in any of our marketing materials. We didn't write it down often. And yet every member of the Digital-Tutors tribe knew why we did what we did: *To improve the lives of our people and the people who use our products.*

The order here of our people—our team—over the people who use our products—our customers—is extremely important. We didn't put our customers first. My role as a business owner was to take care of my core tribe first so that they, in turn, could take care of our larger tribe. I took care of the team. The team took care of the customer. The customer took care of me. After our conversation on that bench in Napa Valley, Dana opened my eyes to the importance of that order.

WORKING MYSELF OUT OF A JOB

For any of my public-facing work at Digital-Tutors, I used the pen name Papa Giorgio. (Only fans of the movie *Vegas Vacation* will get that reference.) Any student or client who took our courses had no idea they were being taught by the owner of Digital-Tutors. They thought I was just another artist-turned-trainer.

Why the fiction?

I didn't want Digital-Tutors to be about me. I wanted to build an organization that was bigger than any one person. Digital-Tutors

We didn't put our customers first. My role as a business owner was to take care of my core tribe first so that they, in turn, could take care of our larger tribe. I took care of the team. The team took care of the customer. The customer took care of me.

was, in many ways, a movement: we were changing the world, one student at a time. For a movement to gain its own momentum, it needs to be about something greater than a single individual.

I achieved bittersweet success: on my last day as CEO, I told my tribe who were staying on with the new owners to call if they needed anything, anything at all. Do you know how many times my phone rang? Not even once. Nobody needed me.

They continued to produce incredible work, week after week, month after month. I'd worked myself out of a job. My former employees were winning championships while their former coach sat at home "watching the game" from his living room.

This is the true meaning of hiring people better than you and trusting them to reach the company's goals. By focusing on values and our vision, the tribe could keep moving and growing without the founder. Digital-Tutors had outgrown me.

YOUR TURN!

That's my challenge for you: start working yourself out of a job. As a business owner, your role isn't to be the glue that holds your company together forever. If so, then as soon as you're gone, your business will be, too. You'll never retire if the business can't go on without you.

That's what I want for you…and here's how to get there:

- **Discover your core values—the rules of your game.**

- **Find ways to continually inject belonging, affirmation, and meaning for your employees.** Commit to the 3 Happies for thirty days.

Start working yourself out of a job.

- **Get input from your tribe.** What should you keep doing? What should you stop doing?

- **Never settle.** Put systems in place to constantly check what you're doing against your values.

- **Hire people who are smarter than you.**

- **Identify people who "get it" and let them mentor your new hires into your tribe.**

- **Help your people find the right seat on the bus; let go of those who don't have one.**

- **Empower your leadership team.** Constantly coach and communicate with them.

- **Get familiar with G.R.O.W.** Practice uncomfortable conversations, and don't be afraid of them.

- **Put systems in place to determine if you're winning or losing.**

- **Keep growing.** Find peers and role models—in books or real life—to help you grow.

- **Focus on the *why* and make sure your tribe knows what it is.**

Although we've reached the end of this book, it's just the beginning of your tribe's story. Transforming your business may take years or, like me, decades. Keeping your tribe successful can be just as difficult. There will be ups and downs. It won't be easy, but you're not alone.

"HEY...DOES THIS STUFF ACTUALLY WORK?"

In year one, I started Digital-Tutors in my living room with $54 dollars and a vision of teaching online in a different way than what was currently practiced. I was working alongside my wife and two of my best friends. By year three, I had an awesome team of people and the company was growing rapidly. By year five, I'd lost my focus and had to be reminded of my *why* and my personal values. By year seven, we were well-established as a global player in the world of visual effects. Year nine was formidable for us. We completely pivoted the company from a physical disc company (shipping our training on CDs) to a one hundred percent online company. Imagine firing all your customers and starting over. By year fourteen, I sold the company for $45 million.

We did this without any debt, investors, or loans. More than financial success, we created a tribe of people that spanned the globe and friendships that endure to this day. Our mission was to change the lives of our employees and the customers who use our products.

We achieved our mission; yes, this stuff works.

I'm just a kid from a small town in Oklahoma. If I can build a company with no experience, so can you. It's your turn to look at your business. It's your dream that's waiting to be realized. It's your team that's waiting to become your tribe.

NOW IT'S REALLY YOUR TURN!

Throughout this book, I've shared my own journey and the tools that helped me. The real challenge begins when you start implementing those tools into your business. As you start that process, there's bound to be questions that arise.

Where do you begin wrapping your head around defining the Rules of Your Game? How can you implement the Three Happies in your company?

I've dedicated the website for this book to be a place to help you answer those questions and more. As you're going down the path of transforming your team into a tribe, I'd encourage you to take advantage of the free tools and resources available on the book's home on the web at leadlovetribe.com.

ABOUT THE AUTHOR

The son of Indian immigrants, Piyush Patel grew up helping his family run their roadside motel in El Reno, Oklahoma. His father ran the front desk and the lawn mower. His mother did everything else, from housekeeping to bookkeeping and caring for the extended family.

After graduating from high school, Piyush entered Oklahoma State University, and earned a bachelor's in elementary education and middle school math and science.

While teaching sixth-graders science, he taught himself digital animation and began moonlighting as an adjunct at a local community college. The college soon hired him full-time to develop a state-of-the art teaching facility for animation. While teaching, he also earned a master's degree in adult education with an emphasis in e-Learning.

Having authored several technical textbooks, he realized that the model of teaching had to change. He recorded a dozen video lessons on how to animate a cartoon character. The day he posted the first videos online, he received an email from a visual effects artist in Israel asking if he could buy the lessons on CD. The artist sent a PayPal payment to cover the shipping—and Digital-Tutors was born.

After quitting his tenured position, Piyush hired his wife and two of his best friends and started working full time building the company. Within five years, the training studio was firmly established in the movie and gaming industry, with clients that included LucasArts, Pixar, Electronic Arts, Blizzard, and Disney—not to mention thousands of individual customers in nearly every country.

In 2014, Piyush received an offer from Pluralsight, based in Salt Lake City, to buy Digital-Tutors for $45 million. After many late-night talks, he and his wife decided it was time for the next adventure. He stayed on for a year to help with the transition before closing that chapter of his life.

Today, Piyush helps entrepreneurs and small business owners create tribal cultures that enable greatness. He also owns a winery in Napa Valley that focuses on creating high-end, limited-production wines. The gross sales go to Oklahoma nonprofit organizations.

Piyush met his wife, Lisa (a Nebraska native), through an eighth-grade school pen pal project. They wrote to each other faithfully for six years before meeting for the first time. They married four years later, and still live happily in Oklahoma City, with their son, Nick.